# Raising Catholic Kids for Their Vocations

# RAISING CATHOLIC KIDS FOR THEIR VOCATIONS

John and Claire Grabowski

TAN Books
Charlotte, North Carolina

Cover design by Caroline K. Green

Cover image:

Library of Congress Control Number: 2019931273

ISBN: 978-1-5051-1376-1

Published in the United States by
TAN Books
PO Box 410487
Charlotte, NC 28241
www.TANBooks.com

Printed in the United States of America

*For Rachel, Rebekah, Paul, Daniel, and Abigail who taught us how to be parents and always forgave us when we failed*

# CONTENTS

# ACKNOWLEDGMENTS

We would like to thank the many people who supported, encouraged, and assisted us in writing this book. The staff at the Word Among Us Press first suggested this book to us, worked with us on its development, and were gracious and professional throughout our dealings with them. We are especially indebted to Patty Mitchell, Beth MacNamara, Cindy Cavnar, and Jeff Smith. When it became clear that our project differed from their vision, they encouraged us to seek another publisher and freely shared the work and effort they had invested in the book to that point.

We are also thankful for the wonderful people at TAN Books who welcomed this project at a fairly advanced stage and worked to expedite its publication. We are grateful to Paul Grabowski (our son who works in marketing for the company), Mara Persic, John Moorehouse (the Acquisitions Editor), and Conor Gallagher (the Publisher) for their enthusiastic reception and support throughout this process.

In addition to the staff at these two fine publishers, we would like to thank Adriene Pedraza and Melanie Danner for many hours of generous proofreading and constructive suggestions on earlier versions of this manuscript. We are grateful to our children for each contributing a short section to this book, for their love and support, and for their Christian witness to us. It is to them that we dedicate this book.

# INTRODUCTION

When we were first contacted by the Word Among Us Press about writing this book, we almost declined the offer. John already had four other book projects lined up and at various stages of completion and thought that one more would be too much. Initially Claire also decided against it, thinking we were being asked to write a work about marriage. We were in the process of finishing one on that topic and there were already so many available. However, when Claire learned the real subject—raising children for their future vocations (particularly marriage)—she said, "We have to write that book!" After some prayerful reconsideration, John agreed.

It seems that Claire's discernment was the right one because everyone we have subsequently told about the project has spoken of the need for such a book or offered some variation of, "You have to write that!" Sometimes God does not leave much doubt about his will in a given situation.

But why is such a book needed? Raising children is something that Christian parents have done for generations. Christian tradition offers much wisdom on how to go about it, from Scripture to the Church Fathers to the lives of the saints. Contemporary psychology also offers many insights which are enormously helpful to both new and experienced parents. With all of these resources available, why another book? For significant reasons.

The situation of Christian families at the beginning of the twenty-first century is different in important respects from that of previous generations. This is due to new emphases in the teaching and ministry of the Church as well as to changes in the culture in which we live. We will discuss these in greater detail in the pages that follow, but it is worth briefly describing some of them here.

The universal call to holiness recovered and reemphasized in the teaching of the Second Vatican Council has led to a greater focus on the role and mission of the laity in the Church. This has caused the Church's pastors to focus more on the life and mission of Christian families. After all, if lay Christians, like clergy and religious, are called to holiness and most lay people marry and raise families, we need to think more fully about what holiness looks like in this state of life. This in turn requires us to consider how best to form persons to enter into such a state and flourish in it as Christians.

Clergy and consecrated religious undergo intense formation before and after their ordination or vows. Those who are married are also entering into a lifelong state in which they are called to grow in holiness and live out their mission as followers of Jesus. The "Pre-Cana" instruction engaged couples receive is not adequate to equip them to respond to this call. Therefore, much of the formation of those who are married must take place before the engagement and after the wedding. This book focuses on the former (from the perspective of children) and the latter (from the perspective of their parents).

At the same time, the culture around us in the Western world has changed in significant ways. It is in many ways a "post-Christian" culture in which the imprint of Christian faith and moral teaching is increasingly receding from public life and social interchange. Many observers also argue that it is increasingly a "post-marriage" culture since fewer people marry, divorce has become commonplace, and the very understanding of what constitutes marriage has been reshaped to accommodate individually specified identities and desires.

In such a culture, Christian parents seeking to raise their children in a way that prepares them to live out the call to holiness in their future marriage or in religious life cannot count on much by way of social support and reinforcement from government or the wider society. Today's parents therefore need to be much more intentional about passing on and forming their children in the faith than parents just a few generations ago. In raising Christian children, they will encounter challenges not faced by their grandparents or even their parents before them.

This book seeks to help equip parents for that increasingly challenging task. We make no claim that it is exhaustive or definitive. We try to distill some of the wisdom of Scripture and the Church's tradition—especially as articulated in the Church's recent teaching on family—and make it accessible to parents and religious educators. We also share some of our own experience as parents, grandparents, godparents, and participants in various forms of marriage and family ministry. As readers will see, this experience is drawn from both our "successes" and our failures. Like Saint Augustine in his *Confessions* and Saint Paul in his struggle with his "thorn in the flesh" (cf. 1 Cor 12:7–10), we have come to see that it is often in our failures and weakness that we can most fully see and appreciate God's mercy, grace, and power in our lives. Through walking with other Christian families, we know that we are not unique in this regard.

Saint John Paul II, at the conclusion of his apostolic exhortation on the family *Familiaris Consortio*, reminds us that even the Holy Family of Jesus, Mary, and Joseph knew their share of challenges and struggles:

> I wish to invoke the protection of the Holy Family of Nazareth. Through God's mysterious design, it was in that family that the Son of God spent long years of a hidden life. It is therefore the prototype and example for all Christian families. It was unique in the world. Its life was passed in anonymity and silence in a little town in Palestine. It underwent trials of poverty, persecution and exile.
>
> It glorified God in an incomparably exalted and pure way. And it will not fail to help Christian families—indeed, all the families in the world—to be faithful to their day-to-day duties, to bear the cares and tribulations of life, to be open and generous to the needs of others, and to fulfill with joy the plan of God in their regard.[1]

---

1 *Familiaris Consortio*, no. 86.

We join our prayers to the intercession of "the pope of the family" and to that of the Holy Family for the readers of this book, that they too may "fulfill with joy the plan of God" in their family life and in forming their children to respond to the Lord's call.

Urbana, MD
December 30, 2018
Feast of the Holy Family

I

# Welcoming Children as God's Gifts

"Certainly sons are a gift from the LORD, the fruit of the womb, a reward," writes the psalmist (Ps 127:3). This idea echoes through the pages of Scripture—children are a gift from God. In biblical culture, having children was seen as a sign of God's blessing or favor. When Rebekah was about to leave her home to marry Isaac, her family spoke this blessing over her: "Sister, may you grow into thousands of myriads; And may your descendants gain possession of the gates of their enemies" (Gn 24:60). The inability to have children was thought of as God withholding his favor or even as a kind of curse. Think of the many stories about women who are unable to conceive—at least for a period of time—in the Bible (Sarah, Rebekah, Rachel, Hannah, Elizabeth). All of these texts bear witness to the basic truth that children are a gift—a blessing.

Part of the reason for this strong affirmation in Scripture is the fact that people in biblical times could more easily see the contribution children made to the welfare of their family. Because the home was where people worked as well as lived, each child made the family economically stronger by helping with the family farm or trade. Male children carried on the family's name. Children were also a family's "social security," as they were the ones who would care for parents when they were sick or elderly (cf. Ex 20:12; Lv 19:32; Mk 7:9–13; 1 Tm 5:4, 8).

In our day there can be many reasons why couples choose to limit the size of their families and exercise what the Church has called "responsible parenthood." Some of these are good reasons and some may not be as good. It takes careful discernment on the part of a couple who have formed their consciences to respond to God's call to them to generously open themselves to the gift of life and children. Sometimes a couple's discernment of God's will can be colored and even skewed by economic and social forces which they do not fully recognize.

In the Western world of the twenty-first century, it has become much harder for us to think of children as gifts. The Industrial Revolution and the ever-increasing expansion of technology have separated work from the home and family life. Parents work outside of the home while children are cared for at home, in day care, or in schools. This economic shift which has occurred over the last century and a half has transformed the way many in our culture think about children. Children can be seen as burdens which drain a couple's resources because raising and educating them is viewed as expensive and time-consuming.[1] Because of fears generated

1 In 2017 the US Department of Agriculture estimated that the cost of raising a child born in 2015 through age 17 in the US at $233,610. Note that this does not include the cost of college. See Mahita Gajanan, "The Cost of Raising a Child Jumps to $233,610," Money, January 9, 2017, http://time.com/money/4629700/child-raising-cost-department-of-agriculture-report/.

by these changes some couples choose to have few children or none at all. Large families can be regarded as strange or even as threats to the future of the planet.

## Reclaiming a Biblical Perspective

In his catecheses which have come to be known as the Theology of the Body, Pope Saint John Paul II charts a way for us to recover the biblical appreciation of children as gifts. In this effort, we first need to understand that the whole existence of the created world is a gift sprung from the generous love of God the Creator. God did not owe us existence but brought us into being and sustains everything in creation so that he can share his love with us. The human person, created in God's image and likeness (see Gn 1:26–28), is a unique expression of his generosity. Of all the creatures of the physical world, only human beings can recognize that their existence is a gift and acknowledge that gift through praise, worship, and obedience to the Creator. The human person is therefore, in a unique way, a gift who finds fulfillment in the gift of self in love.[2] As Saint John Paul II expressed it: "The person is unique and unrepeatable, someone chosen by eternal Love. The affirmation of the person is nothing but acceptance of the gift, which, by means of reciprocity, creates the communion of persons."[3]

---

2 See John Paul II, Weekly General Audiences of January 2 and January 16, 1980.

3 John Paul II, weekly General Audience of January 16, 1980, https://w2.vatican.va/content/john-paul-ii/en/audiences/1980/documents/hf_jp-ii_aud_19800116.html.

Our bodies, as male and female, bear witness to this call to make a gift of ourselves not just to God but to one another in the communion of love. Saint John Paul II understood that the meaning of our bodies as male or female is found in relation to one another. Masculinity reveals the meaning of femininity, and femininity reveals the meaning of masculinity. Sexual difference is therefore relational or, to use Pope John Paul II's term, "spousal."[4] It is the basis of the sexual self-gift proper to marriage which is a reflection and enactment of the promise at the heart of the marriage covenant. Children are a unique sign and fruit of this giving in love at the heart of marriage.

In the communion of love which is marriage, the fruitfulness of the couple's love reflects the eternal communion of Persons among the Father, Son, and Holy Spirit. From all eternity, God the Father pours himself into his consubstantial Son in an act of generous love. The Son perfectly reflects the Father as his Word and Image and gives himself in love to the Father. The Holy Spirit is breathed forth by both of them as the Gift of their mutual love and the perfection of their mutual communion. This eternal communion of love finds a created analogy and reflection in the fruitfulness of the love between husband and wife which is realized in the person of their child.[5]

The first command God gives to humanity in Scripture occurs in its opening chapter: "God blessed them and God

4 See Pope John Paul II, Weekly General Audience of January 9, 1980.

5 See Pope John Paul II, apostolic letter *Mulieris Dignitatem*, no. 7 and Letter to Families, *Gratissimam Sane*, nos. 6–7.

said to them: Be fruitful and multiply; and fill the earth and subdue it" (Gn 1:28). Note that the command is also a blessing. In biblical Hebrew when God blesses (the verb is *barek*) something, it becomes a source of life. Hence, in the first story of creation (1:1–2:4a), animal life (1:22), the union of man and woman (1:28), and the Sabbath day (2:3) are all blessed by God and become sources of life within creation.

## Cultivating Generosity and Love

It is not enough to simply hold a different point of view about children than the one held by the culture around us. We need to push back against views that devalue children or reduce them to instruments for the happiness of their parents. Speaking of the poverty of wealthy countries where fear of children leads to abortion, Saint Teresa of Calcutta said simply, "A child is a gift from God."[6] Accepting the gift of children enriches our families. One of the greatest gifts we can give to our children are siblings. We are called to cultivate generosity in welcoming children as God's gifts.

Saint John Paul II taught that each child who comes into the world is a "renewal of the mystery of creation" because he or she is a tangible sign of the creative love which brought the world into being.[7] Procreation in marriage is therefore a

6 The full quote is: "It is very painful to accept what is happening in Western countries: a child is destroyed by the fear of having too many children and having to feed or educate it. I think that they are the poorest people in the world who do an act like that. A child is a gift from God." Mother Teresa of Calcutta, *My Life for the Poor*, ed. José Luis González-Balado and Janet N. Playfoot (San Francisco: Harper & Row, 1985), p. 61.

7 Weekly General Audience of April 30, 1980.

form of co-creation. Couples cooperate with God and his plan for the world when they welcome children. He wrote:

> With the creation of man and woman in his own image and likeness, God crowns and brings to perfection the work of his hands: He calls them to a special sharing in his love and in his power as creator and Father through their free and responsible cooperation in transmitting the gift of human life. . . .Thus the fundamental task of the family is to serve life, to actualize in history the original blessing of the creator—that of transmitting by procreation the divine image from person to person.[8]

Parents are entrusted with a unique mission from God—continuing his work of creation in order to make visible and share his love in the world. Cultivating generosity in welcoming the gift of children is an important witness in our culture, which is increasingly confused about children. As Pope Francis has observed, "Large families are a joy for the Church. They are an expression of the fruitfulness of love."[9]

Seeing children as gifts from God and welcoming them into our lives is the foundation of our being able to love them. We were created to be loved by God, to share his love, and ultimately to get to heaven to share eternity with him: "For God so loved the world that he gave his only Son, so that everyone who believes in him might not perish but might have eternal life" (Jn 3:16). As parents, we are called

---

8 John Paul II, apostolic exhortation *Familiaris Consortio*, no. 28.

9 Francis, apostolic exhortation *Amoris Laetitia*, no. 167.

to love our children with that divine love made visible in the cross and poured into our hearts through the Holy Spirit (cf. Rom 5:5–8).

## Growing into Parenthood

Both of us were the youngest of four children by a significant margin (six years for Claire, eight for John) and so never experienced having a baby in the house or siblings close to our own age. We knew, however, that we wanted a large family. For John, this was a more abstract idea. For Claire, it was an extension of her love for children. As a teen, she did a lot of babysitting and worked in summer camps. In college, she was an elementary education major so that she could work with children.

We got married two weeks before we graduated from college. At that point, John, in particular, had reservations about starting a family. This was based in part on a fear of the unknown and in part on worry over our ability to handle the financial expense as a graduate student and a Catholic grade school teacher. We thought that after John finished graduate school and had a "real job" (to use Claire's term), we might be ready for parenthood. We were probably internalizing some of the fear of children in the culture around us. We planned to wait to have children, but God had other—and far better—plans for us. Our first child was born just weeks before our first anniversary. It is difficult to describe what joy she brought into our lives and how she changed the way we understood ourselves from being a couple into being a family.

Studying Scripture and Church teaching began to open our minds and hearts, but what really changed our outlook was actually having children of our own and discovering what a joy they were in themselves and in how they transformed and deepened our marriage. As Saint Zélie Martin explains in a letter to her daughter Pauline:

> When we had our children, our ideas changed somewhat. Thereafter we lived only for them; they made all our happiness and we would have never found it save in them. In fact, nothing any longer cost us anything; the world was no longer a burden to us. As for me, my children were my great compensation, so that I wished to have many in order to bring them up for heaven.[10]

That was our experience as new parents as well—wanting nothing more than to let our daughter know how much she was loved by God and by us.

This first pregnancy was difficult for Claire, but nevertheless we wanted to have another child as soon as possible. Once again, we found that our plans were not the same as God's plans—we had difficulty achieving a second pregnancy. It wasn't until three years later—and after learning a different method of Natural Family Planning (NFP) to help us conceive—that our second daughter was born. This experience brought home to us the reality that children are a gift from God and that we cannot just decide when we will have them. Ultimately, God is the author of life.

---

10 Cited in Stéfane Jospeh Piat, O.F.M. *The Story of a Family: The Home of St. Thérèse of Lisieux*, trans. by a monk of Stanbrook Abbey (Charlotte, NC: TAN Books, 2015), p. 48.

We had planned on a large family with children born close together. We ended up being blessed with five children, with the last coming six years after the fourth. Each one is a gift from God with a unique personality and gifts which have enriched our family. Families shape their children, but each child is also a gift to parents and siblings, bringing new joys and challenges.[11]

## What About Adoption?

But what about couples who are unable to have children of their own? Infertility is a cross which affects many marriages.[12] As we saw, it impacted couples in biblical times. It also affected couples in the early Church. Saint John Chrysostom, the great preacher of the fourth-century Christian East, says in one of his homilies:

> The child is a sort of bridge connecting the mother to the father, so that the three become one flesh, as when two cities divided by a river are joined by a bridge. But suppose there is no child; do they remain two and not one? No, their intercourse effects the joining of their bodies, and they are made one, just as when perfume is mixed with ointment.[13]

---

11 Cf. Pope John Paul II, Letter to Families, *Gratissimam Sane*, nos. 9–10.

12 For a good overview of the reality of infertility, Catholic teaching, and the spiritual needs of couples dealing with this challenge, see Carmen Santamaria and Angelique Ruhi-Lopez, *The Infertility Companion for Catholics: Spiritual and Practical Support for Couples* (Notre Dame, IN: Ave Maria Press, 2012).

13 Saint John Chrysostom, "Homily 12 on Col. 4:18," cited in *On*

It seems that his experience as a pastor in Antioch and Constantinople had brought him into contact with couples who were unable to conceive a child, and so he sought to reassure such couples of the reality of their marital union.

Throughout Christian history, adoption has been one of the distinctive practices that set followers of Jesus apart from their neighbors. Saint Paul described Gentile Christians as adopted children of God, grafted into God's covenant relationship with the chosen people of Israel (cf. Rom 8:14–16). Early Christians who rescued and adopted children abandoned by pagan Roman families saw this practice as an extension of the same love which God had shown them in Christ. Today, adoption remains another way for couples to express the fruitfulness of their love. As Pope Francis teaches:

> Adoption is a very generous way to become parents. I encourage those who cannot have children to expand their marital love to embrace those who lack a proper family situation. They will never regret having been generous. Adopting a child is an act of love, offering the gift of a family to someone who has none.
>
> It is important to insist that legislation help facilitate the adoption process, above all in the case of unwanted children, in order to prevent their abortion or abandonment. Those who accept the challenge of adopting and accepting someone unconditionally and gratuitously become channels of God's love.[14]

---

*Marriage and Family Life*, ed. Catherine Roth (Crestwood, NY: Saint Vladimir's Seminary Press, 1986), p. 76.

14 *Amoris Laetitia,* no. 179.

This act of generosity can be undertaken both by couples who experience infertility and those who do not but who simply want to share their home and family with a child who needs them.

Adoption is not a "second class" way for a couple to become parents. In Scripture, when two parties enter into a covenant, they enter into the same type of bond that exists between blood relations. Thus in Exodus 24 after the people agree to the terms of their covenant with God, Moses takes the blood of sacrificed animals and sprinkles some on the altar (symbolizing God) and some on the people (Ex 24:3–8). Blood in the Bible was understood as a symbol of life and therefore belonged to God who is the author of life (cf. Lv 17:10–14). Hence this covenant ratification ceremony at Mt. Sinai indicates that God and the people of Israel share a common life—that is, they are family. When a couple enters into the covenant of marriage, they become "one flesh" (Gn 2:24). When a couple adopts a child, they are, in effect, making a covenant with that child. They bind themselves to the child, promising their unconditional love and care. In doing so, they become the child's parents as truly as if the child was biologically their own.

Although we do not have direct experience of adoption ourselves, we have many friends who have adopted one, two, to as many as six, children. The children in all these families are loved and cherished as children of God. These parents and children believe that each member of their family is special and a gift from God and that God is the one who brought their family together.

Whether our children come to us through birth or adoption, learning to see them as gifts of God and welcoming them with generosity is the seedbed for cultivating love in our hearts and our homes. The first and most important gift we give our children is love. They come to know and experience God's love through us—their parents. It is only in knowing that we are loved by our parents and by God that we can begin to trust, to believe that we were created for a purpose—to love and serve God. It is in trusting God that we can open ourselves to his plan for our lives. For our children, that plan includes their future vocation—the best path for them in coming to know God's love and sharing that love with others.

**Key Points**

- Scripture and Church teaching help us understand that children are a gift and a blessing.
- As married couples, we are called to cultivate generous openness to the gift of children.
- This generous love is the foundation of our being able to raise and care for children.
- Adopted children are likewise gifts from God and are bound to their parents in a covenant as real as a blood relation.

2

# Face to Face

Modern scholars tell us that the Bible itself does not use the term *person* as we have come to understand it to describe either God or human beings made in his image. Instead, the ideas of individual uniqueness, dignity, and being in relation, which are at the heart of our understanding of personhood, are conveyed in other ways. Through these means, God reveals himself as personal—in fact, as a communion of Persons—in Scripture. By doing so, God enables us to understand ourselves more deeply. Two of these are the concepts of a "face" and a "name." This chapter focuses on the first of these.

### The Face of God and the Faces of Men

Though God is a spiritual Being (cf. Jn 4:24), the Scriptures are full of references to his "face" (Hebrew *panim*; Greek *prosópon*). When God "hides his face," he withholds his blessing (cf. Ps 13:1; 44:24; 88:14) or is angry with his people (see Is 54:8; Jer 33:5). To "seek God's face" is to strive to come to know him through prayer and repentance (see 2 Chr 7:14; 33:12) or to worship before him in the temple (Ps 42:3). The angels in heaven see God's face (Mt 18:1), and so will the righteous in heaven who have been perfected in love (see 1 Cor 13: 12; cf. Rv 22:4). The concept of God's "face" thus gives an insight into who he is and how he relates to us—that is, it discloses his love and holiness.

In the same way, the human face is a window into who we are as persons—or in biblical parlance, our hearts. "As face mirrors face in water, so the heart reflects the person" (Prv 27:19), says the sage. The face displays the emotions that move within a person's heart—whether anguish (cf. Jer 30:6; Is 13:8), exhaustion (cf. Dn 1:10), or the light of joy (cf. Prv 15:13). It should be remembered that "the heart" (Hebrew *leb;* Greek *kardia*) in the Bible is more than just the seat of feelings or emotions. It is the spiritual center of the person—encompassing the intellect and will as well as the spiritual capacity to hear the voice of God speaking to us (cf. Ps 96:7–8; Heb 3:15). Thus the human face, too, gives us a glimpse into the depths of the person and his or her character.

At the center of the biblical revelation of God's character or "personality" is his holiness. It is for this reason that some biblical texts reflect the idea that humans cannot see the face of God and live (see Jgs 13:22; Ex 33:20). Simply to enter God's presence brings fear because of our human sinfulness. The prophet Isaiah, seeing a vision of God seated on his throne, exclaims, "'Woe is me, I am doomed! For I am a man of unclean lips, living among a people of unclean lips, and my eyes have seen the King, the LORD of hosts!'" (Is 6:5). Yet Isaiah survives this awesome encounter, and his sin is purged by God's mercy (see Is 6:6–7).

Moses is said to have spoken to God "face to face, as a person speaks to a friend" (Ex 33:11). However, when he asks to see God's glory, he is only able to see his back (see Ex 33:18–23). After encountering the Lord's glory on the mountain, Moses's face is set aglow: "As Moses came down from Mount Sinai with the two tablets of the covenant in his hands, he did not know that the skin of his face had become radiant while he spoke with the LORD" (Ex 34:29).

What is true of Moses is even more true of the New Moses. In Jesus, we see the face of the Father shining even more brilliantly (cf. 2 Cor 4:6). In the Gospels, this glory is visualized for us in the accounts of the Transfiguration (see Mk 9:2–8; Mt 17:1–8; Lk 9:28–36; 2 Pt 1:16–18). In it, Jesus's face "shone like the sun and his clothes became white as light" (Mt 17:2), and the Father's voice declares, "This is my beloved Son, with whom I am well pleased; listen to him" (Mt 17:5). In this event, the glory of Jesus's divinity which he shares with the Father and with the Holy Spirit shines through his humanity.

The glory here described in the Gospels is not just that of a past event. In faith, we too can gaze upon the face of the Lord and be transformed. St. Paul declares, "All of us, gazing with unveiled face on the glory of the Lord, are being transformed into the same image from glory to glory, as from the Lord who is the Spirit" (2 Cor 3:18). Encountering Jesus and his glory transforms our personality and enables us to become what Saint Paul calls "spiritual persons" (cf. 1 Cor 2:10–16) who live "life in the Spirit"; that is, the Christian life.

### The Face of the Unborn and the Newborn

For couples expecting a child, pregnancy is a time of waiting and expectation. Couples dream about what the child growing within the mother will be like—what kind of temperament and gifts will he or she have? What does the future hold? Women are the first to bond with the child during pregnancy, sharing their bodies with their unborn child and feeling his or her movement within them. As Pope Francis observes:

> Pregnancy is a difficult but wonderful time. A mother joins with God to bring forth the miracle of a new life. Motherhood is the fruit of a "particular creative potential of the female body, directed to the conception and birth of a new human being." Each woman shares in "the mystery of creation, which is renewed with each birth."
>
> The Psalmist says: "You knit me together in my mother's womb" (Ps 139:13). Every child growing within the mother's womb is part of the eternal loving plan of God the Father: "Before I formed you in the womb I knew you, and before you were born I consecrated you" (Jer 1:5). Each child has a place in God's heart from all eternity; once he or she is conceived, the Creator's eternal dream comes true.[1]

The bonds between parents and child are formed before birth. Scientists tell us that communication between unborn

---

1 *Amoris Laetitia*, no. 168.

children and the mothers who carry them takes place on numerous levels—from chemical messages to each other's bodies, to touch and movement, to hearing, and even senses like taste and sight.[2] Fathers remain someone outside of this process and so, as Pope St. John Paul II observed, have to learn how to enter into this growing bond: "The man—even with his sharing in parenthood—always remains 'outside' the process of pregnancy and the baby's birth; in many ways he has to learn his own 'fatherhood' from the mother."[3] Through their baby's movements, the couple might get inklings of their child's temperament and personality, an ultrasound might enable them to catch glimpses of the unborn person, but parents and child still remain in some ways in the dark regarding one another.

It is at birth that parents see the face of their child for the first time. The pain and fear of labor recedes in the excitement of seeing the newborn child. As Jesus tells his apostles, "When a woman is in labor, she is in anguish because her hour has arrived; but when she has given birth to a child, she no longer remembers the pain because of her joy that a child has been born into the world" (Jn 16:21). Now parents and child begin to know one another and bond in new and deeper ways. Mothers' bonds with their children, begun during pregnancy, are biochemically reinforced during labor

---

2 See, for example, Shawn A. Tassone, "The Two-Way Umbilical Cord: Bonding with Your Baby Before Birth," *The Llewellyn Journal*, accessed June 15, 2017, https://www.llewellyn.com/journal/article/2421.

3 Pope John Paul II, apostolic letter *Mulieris Dignitatem*, no. 18.

and breastfeeding.[4] Fathers can begin bonding with their children in a new and deeper way as well, especially through physical touch such as holding them. For both parents, the experience of seeing their child's face is an important moment of connection. In that new little face, we see the uniqueness of the child given to us by God, characteristics of the two families represented, and hints of the child's future personality.

Faces are important for babies too. Babies are born with limited ability to see and to focus. As their vision sharpens, one of the first things that they can focus on are faces of those who care for them. This is crucial to their developing a sense of themselves as a self—an "I." Infants don't distinguish their awareness of themselves from their awareness of the world around them. And so when a baby is wet, the world is wet. When a baby is hungry, the world is hungry. The baby's usual response to the wetness or hunger of the world is to cry. But over time, the baby realizes that when the world is wet or hungry, a face comes and then the world stops being wet and hungry. So the child comes to recognize that he or she is not the whole world but only a part of it. The child's recognition of himself as a self is therefore dependent upon recognizing the otherness of others—for there to be an "I" there must be a "You" (or a "Thou" in the language of some modern philosophers). The faces of the child's parents, along with the love and care they show, are a

4 See, for example, Linda F. Palmer, "Bonding Matters . . . The Chemistry of Attachment," August 6, 2013, http://babyreference.com/bonding-matters-the-chemistry-of-attachment/.

key part of this formation of the baby's self-concept which is a foundation for his or her personality.

This love and care expressed through the faces and the touch of their parents also lays a foundation for the child to encounter and experience the love of God. In fact, it is a concrete manifestation of that love. As Pope Francis teaches:

> Children, once born, begin to receive, along with nourishment and care, the spiritual gift of knowing with certainty that they are loved. This love is shown to them through the gift of their personal name, the sharing of language, looks of love, and the brightness of a smile. In this way, they learn that the beauty of human relationships touches our soul, seeks our freedom, accepts the difference of others, recognizes and respects them as a partner in dialogue. . . . Such is love, and it contains a spark of God's love![5]

## The Faces of Our Children

Just four months after we were married, we discovered we were pregnant with our first child. We were filled with anticipation and fear, not knowing how this child was going to change our lives. Even before realizing that she was pregnant, Claire felt different. After learning that we were expecting, friends reassured us that it was good to have morning sickness because it meant that Claire's hormones were doing the right things. Had they not offered this encouragement, we would have thought that there was something terribly wrong

---

5 *Amoris Laetitia*, no. 172 (citing his own catechesis of October 14, 2015).

with her because she felt awful for nine months. "Morning sickness" was an all-day and all-pregnancy phenomenon with our first. The amazing thing was that immediately after giving birth, Claire felt wonderful and could honestly say that she wanted to do it again.

One of the most exciting things for both of us during pregnancy was feeling our children move within Claire. We did not find out the sex of our children before their birth with the first four, but somehow, without the aid of medical assistance, Claire knew their sex before they were born. She knew that our first child was a girl. As the baby moved within her, Claire would have John put his hand on her stomach to feel her move and kick. One evening, we went to a Christian concert and the baby began jumping and dancing inside of her in time with the music. We constantly spoke to the baby, telling her that we loved her and how we could not wait to meet her.

Because Claire was always feeling sick, when she was not working, she spent a lot of time lying down and so John would read to her and the baby. John had been a fan of Tolkein's work since his childhood, and so while Claire rested, he read the entire *Lord of the Rings* trilogy to her, finishing in the labor and delivery room. To this day, our daughter Rachel is an avid reader, has read through the trilogy some twenty times, and has taken advanced degrees in medieval studies—the wellspring of Tolkien's scholarship and imagination. We have no doubt that the seeds of her interest were planted while she was still in the womb.

Our youngest child was born six years after her closest sibling. She was doted on by her parents and her older siblings.

Her two older sisters were present in the delivery room. This was the culmination of a year of homeschooling science class in which they studied the development of unborn children. It was certainly a learning experience for them, but what struck us was the joy on their faces when they saw the face of their baby sister and were able to hold her for the first time. We learned that bonding is not something that happens only between parents and children.

In spite of the fact that we raised them in largely the same way, each of our children is very different. This was apparent as they came into the world. Each presented differently at birth: one was born "sunny side up," another was born breach and dislocated a hip in the process; the next came into the world fast and hard; while another was an emergency C-section. Our last child was an induced labor who had to be manually turned out of a breach presentation and then Claire's labor restarted. They looked different as well—one was born with a head full of dark hair, others were born with light brown or even blond hair, while one was nearly bald. But it was their faces which captured us—each alike and yet different, with hints of one side of the family or the other. And as they grew and their distinct personalities emerged, they "grew into" their faces and we came to identify the one with the other.

We still are amazed that children born from the same parents and raised in the same house could be as different as ours are. One was a people-pleaser and an over-achiever, another was determined to do everything her way and made it clear to everyone around her—by her expressions even before she could talk. Our boys were easy going but adventuresome, always trying to do everything their big sisters did. They played with their sisters' toys, but it was very evident that they were different from them when they picked up their dolls and began a sword fight with them. One child loved music and could hum a tune before he could talk. His brother had no fear and was climbing and jumping off things as soon as he could walk—the higher, the better. One boy loved to dress up as a knight or a cowboy, while the other would not wear a costume even on Halloween or All Saints Day.

Oh, how different each one was—and is! We have scholars, athletes, and artists, introverts and extroverts, and those who are a bit of both. At family get-togethers and in family photos with our now adult children, we can see family resemblance and distinctive personalities written in every face.

## The Face of Jesus

Pope Francis introduced the Jubilee Year of Mercy in his pontificate by proclaiming, "Jesus Christ is the face of the Father's mercy. These words might well sum up the mystery of the Christian faith. Mercy has become living and visible in Jesus of Nazareth, reaching its culmination in him."[6] God the Father is not the angry, distant, punishing Being imagined by some, but rather is "rich in mercy" (Eph 2:4), and this is fully revealed in the Person of his divine Son. As Pope Francis explains further, "Whoever sees Jesus sees the Father

---

6 Francis, papal bull *Misericordiea Vultus*, no. 1.

(cf. Jn 14:9). Jesus of Nazareth, by his words, his actions, and his entire person reveals the mercy of God."[7]

Our most important task as Christian parents is to enable our children to encounter the person of Jesus. Pope Francis notes that the bishops of the 2015 Synod on family began with the merciful gaze of Jesus, speaking of how he "looked upon the women and men whom he met with love and tenderness, accompanying their steps in truth, patience and mercy as he proclaimed the demands of the Kingdom of God."[8] We need to create opportunities for our children to encounter this gaze of mercy and love in the face of the Lord.

Sometimes we hear parents say that they don't want to force their Christian beliefs on their children but rather give them freedom to choose for themselves what to believe. The argument is specious. God's merciful love never overwhelms or overrides our freedom but rather heals and liberates it. In the account of the meeting between Jesus and the rich young man in Mark's Gospel, Mark tells us that after the young man had informed the Lord that he had kept the commandments from his youth, "Jesus, looking at him, loved him" (Mk 10:21) and then invited him to sell his belongings, give the money to the poor, and follow him as a disciple. St. John Paul II, in his commentary on this passage, makes clear that saying yes to the call to follow Jesus is made possible not by human effort but by the gift of God's grace and love.[9] Note that though the young man was offered this gift by the Lord who loved him, "his face fell, and he went away sad, for he

---

7 Ibid.

8 *Amoris Laetitia*, no. 60.

9 See encyclical *Veritatis Splendor*, no. 17.

had many possessions" (v. 22). We can always reject God's love and mercy. But if we don't encounter Jesus who is the face of the Father's mercy, we don't have the opportunity to say yes to the gift of faith which he offers.

This is the opportunity we must create for our children—not on a one-time basis, but consistently over time, inside and outside of our homes. As Christians, we are called to encounter the Lord every day. As Pope Francis exhorts us: "I invite all Christians, everywhere, at this very moment, to a renewed personal encounter with Jesus Christ, or at least an openness to letting him encounter them; I ask all of you to do this unfailingly each day. No one should think that this invitation is not meant for him or her, since 'no one is excluded from the joy brought by the Lord.'"[10]

Parents are called to bring their children to this encounter—in the Church's sacramental worship, in family prayer, in passing on the faith to their children, in the daily life and practices of their homes. In this way, children can receive from the Lord that "look of love" and the invitation to follow him. Through Jesus they come to know God the Father who is rich in mercy.

### Key Points

- In Scripture, "the face" is a window into the reality of the person—both divine and human.
- Seeing a child's face for the first time is a key moment in family bonding.
- Jesus reveals to us the face of the Father's mercy and love.

---

10 Francis, apostolic exhortation *Evangelli Gaudium,* no. 3.

- One of our key tasks as parents is to lead our children to encounter Jesus "face to face" throughout their lives.

3

# What's in a Name?

The other way in which the Bible articulates the idea of the uniqueness and individuality of the person is through the concept of names. In the second story of creation in Genesis, after God creates the man and places him in the Garden of Eden as its steward, God fashions various animals and leads them to the man to receive names: "So the LORD God formed out of the ground all the wild animals and all the birds of the air, and he brought them to the man to see what he would call them; whatever the man called each living creature was then its name. The man gave names to all the tame animals, all the birds of the air, and all the wild animals; but none proved to be a helper suited to the man" (Gn 2:19–20).

To be able to give a name to a thing is a sign of authority in the Bible. One can grasp the essence of a thing and express it in words. Note that even God accepts the names given by the man to his fellow creatures—a further sign of man's dominion in creation, having been created in "the image of God" (cf. Gn 1:26–28).

Names also give insight into the nature of the person, and so knowing them is a sign of trust and intimacy—particularly the name of God. It is for this reason that Moses seeks to know God's name when being sent to lead the people of Israel out of their captivity in Egypt: "'But,' said Moses to God, 'if I go to the Israelites and say to them, "The God of your ancestors has sent me to you," and they ask me, "What is his name?" what do I tell them?' God replied to Moses: I am who I am. Then he added: This is what you will tell the Israelites: I AM has sent me to you" (Ex 3: 13–14).

For Moses, knowing God's proper name was a sign that he was in God's confidence and spoke on his behalf. Knowing God's proper name, *Yahweh,* was precious to the people of Israel. Out of reverence for this name, they would typically not write it or even read it aloud, substituting "the Lord" (Hebrew *Adonai*) in its place.[1] Because the name of God communicates his nature and holiness, misuse of it was understood as a sin which violated the Decalogue which stood at the heart of Israel's covenant with Yahweh (cf. Ex 20:7; Dt 5:11).

As Christians, we are baptized in the name of the Father, the Son, and the Holy Spirit (cf. Mt 28:19), indicating our dignity and the depth of the new relationship we have as adopted children of God. The *Catechism of the Catholic Church* succinctly summarizes some of the primary effects of being baptized in the name of the Trinity:

---

1 The term *Jehovah* is actually a mistranslation which resulted from combining the consonants of YHWH with the vowel points of *Adonai*, written in the text to remind those reading it to say "the Lord" instead of pronouncing God's proper name. In the original Hebrew, the term has no meaning.

> Baptism not only purifies from all sins, but also makes the neophyte "a new creature," an adopted son of God, who has become a "partaker of the divine nature," member of Christ and co-heir with him, and a temple of the Holy Spirit. The Most Holy Trinity gives the baptized sanctifying grace, the grace of justification:
>
> - enabling them to believe in God, to hope in him, and to love him through the theological virtues;
>
> - giving them the power to live and act under the prompting of the Holy Spirit through the gifts of the Holy Spirit;
>
> - allowing them to grow in goodness through the moral virtues.
>
> Thus the whole organism of the Christian's supernatural life has its roots in Baptism.
>
> Baptism makes us members of the Body of Christ: "Therefore . . . we are members one of another." Baptism incorporates us *into the Church*.[2]

Scripture shows us that there is significance in our names as well. The fact that God knows our names is a sign of his intimate love and care for us: "But now, thus says the LORD, who created you, Jacob, and formed you, Israel: Do not fear, for I have redeemed you; I have called you by name: you are mine" (Is 43:1). When God calls someone or gives them a particular task, he sometimes changes their name. Abram (high father) and Sarai (my princess) who are promised a land, numerous descendants, and are blessed with a child

---

2 CCC 1265–67.

in their old age, are renamed Abraham (father of a multitude) and Sarah (mother of nations) by God. Their grandson Jacob is renamed Israel and is the father of the twelve tribes that comprise the nation of that name. In the New Testament, Simon becomes Peter, "the rock" on whom the Church would be built. Saul the persecutor of the Church becomes Paul, the apostle to the Gentiles.

## Naming Children

Sometimes couples who are expecting will not discuss their ideas for names with friends or especially with others in their families out of a fear that someone will "steal" or criticize their baby names. This is unfortunate because it can indicate a fundamental lack of trust among people who should be close. But even more, it shows an insufficient understanding of the role God plays in this process. In his infinite wisdom, God knows the name we will choose for our children—and honors the choice of names by using them for all eternity. As Pope Francis tells us, "The gift of a new child, entrusted by the Lord to a father and a mother, begins with acceptance, continues with lifelong protection and has as its final goal the joy of eternal life. By serenely contemplating the ultimate fulfilment of each human person, parents will be even more aware of the precious gift entrusted to them. For God allows parents to choose the name by which he himself will call their child for all eternity."[3]

The fact that God uses the names we give our children is a sign of our responsibility as parents. Ultimately, our children

---

3 *Amoris Laetitia*, no. 166.

belong to God more than to us—we simply cooperate with his plan in bringing them into the world and leading them to him.

The Church recommends including a saint's name or a Christian mystery (for example, Faith, Pascal, or Immaculata) when naming a child. In this vein, Pope Benedict XVI noted, "Not by chance, in fact, does every baptized person acquire the character of son, based on the Christian name, an unmistakable sign that the Holy Spirit gives birth to man 'anew' from the womb of the Church."[4] This is a permanent sign of the Christian dignity given in baptism. Pope Benedict continued:

> Baptism is the beginning of the spiritual life which finds its fullness in the Church. At the favorable moment of the sacrament, while the ecclesial community is praying and entrusting to God a new son or daughter, parents and godparents commit themselves to welcoming the newly baptized, sustaining them in Christian formation and education.
>
> This is a great responsibility which comes from a great gift! Therefore, I desire to encourage all the faithful to rediscover the beauty of being baptized and of belonging to the large family of God, and to give a joyful witness of their faith so that this faith may produce fruits of good and harmony.[5]

---

4 Angelus Message, January 9, 2011.

5 Ibid.

Parents who name their children after saints give them models of the Christian life to emulate. As children learn about their saint, they can develop relationships with these powerful heavenly intercessors that can deepen over a lifetime. In a similar way, children named after a Christian mystery should come to understand their name's origin and what it signifies. Parents can also find it helpful to recall and celebrate the date of their child's baptism so that they can commemorate not just the physical birth but the date of rebirth in Christ.

Taking names plays an important role in the life of the Church as well. Young people are encouraged to take another Christian name at their confirmation when they are sealed by the Holy Spirit to take up their mission as mature disciples of Jesus. When men and women enter religious life, they take a new name, signifying their new identity within their community. The book of Revelation describes the redeemed in heaven receiving a white amulet or stone with a new name, indicating the perfecting of their identity as sons and daughters of God reborn in Christ (cf. Rv 2:17). Therefore, names point us toward our vocation as Christians and the ways in which we are called to live it out.

## Naming Our Children

Once we were engaged, we began to try to imagine our future life together. Among the things we discussed were the names of our future children. We were drawn to biblical names and to saints' names, and in conversation together, we identified names which resonated with both of us. Learning what various names meant helped with this process of winnowing and selection. Over time and with prayer, the names became clear as the children came to us—for the first four, Rachel Elizabeth, Rebekah Anne, Paul Stephen, and Daniel John. We had their names picked out before entering the delivery room.

Some six years later to our great happiness, we found ourselves pregnant again, and we prayed about and discussed names with our older children. In part so that we could have these conversations with our other children, we broke with our earlier practice and learned the sex of the child Claire was carrying. We attended a sonogram as a family and discovered that we had another daughter on the way. Much of our family prayer and discussion for many days revolved around possible names. We finally settled on Abigail when we learned what it meant. The name comes from two Hebrew words: *ab* ("father") and *giyl* ("rejoicing"). We truly felt that God the Father rejoiced that we were having another child. We have reminded her of this many times over the years (sometimes to her exasperation). We have also had to remind ourselves of this etymology at those inevitable moments of parenthood when we've been less than happy with her.

In her case we coupled this biblical name with a Christian mystery rather than a saint for a middle name—Grace. We did this because we believed that having another child after some years of trying was a gift—one of the meanings of the term *grace* (Hebrew *chen*; Greek *charis*) is precisely that of gratuity. We also chose it because it denotes the life God communicates to us and reminded us of our calling as parents to nurture that life in our daughter.

Learning about the meaning of their names meant reading many Bible stories and lives of the saints to our children. As they grew older, they continued this reading on their own, reading not just about their patrons but about many other saints as well. It was this wide reading among the lives of the saints that enabled our children to select their confirmation names—Joan (of Arc), Catherine (of Sienna), Andrew (the apostle), Francis (of Assisi), Thérèse (of Lisieux)—to begin relationships with new patrons to guide them as adult Christians. This also gave us additional feast days to celebrate which was a way to acknowledge our children and their relationships with these heavenly patrons.

### Key Points

- In Scripture, a name is understood to communicate the essence of a thing, a person, or a person's vocation.
- As Christians, we are baptized in the name of the Father, the Son, and the Holy Spirit.
- God honors the names which parents give their children.
- The Church encourages parents to give their children the name of a saint or a Christian mystery.

4

# Fanning the Flame: The Gift of Faith

Faith is born of the encounter with Christ. As Pope Francis teaches, "The truth which faith discloses to us is a truth centered on the encounter with Christ."[1] For many Christians and for most Catholics, this encounter first takes place in the sacrament of Baptism. As noted in the previous chapter, Baptism has numerous effects. Among the most important is that it communicates God's life to us. God, in the Person of the Holy Spirit, begins to live in the soul of the newly baptized. Living in the soul of the neophyte, the Holy Spirit infuses into him or her the theological virtues of faith, hope, and love. These virtues order us to God and give us the capacity for a relationship with him that we do not possess on our own. That is to say, these virtues are gifts from God—they are not products of our own effort or will. We cannot create the virtues of faith, hope, or love in ourselves or in others. We can only receive them from God.

Nonetheless, we can foster and cooperate with these gifts in ways that assist their growth and development. Thus Saint

1 Francis, encyclical *Lumen Fidei*, no. 30.

Paul says to his disciple Timothy, "I recall your sincere faith that first lived in your grandmother Lois and in your mother Eunice and that I am confident lives also in you. For this reason, I remind you to stir into flame the gift of God that you have through the imposition of my hands" (2 Tm 1:5–6). Faith is here likened to a flame produced in the Christian by the Holy Spirit. And like a fire, faith can be tended or "stirred" so as to make it stronger.

This image for faith as a flame is present in the baptismal liturgy itself in the symbol of the lit candle. After the child is baptized, a small candle is ignited from the Easter candle which symbolizes the Risen Christ to whom the child has been united in baptism (cf. Rom 6:3–11). The celebrant of the rite (bishop, priest, or deacon) then says to the parents and godparents: "Parents and godparents, this light is entrusted to you to be kept burning brightly. This child of yours has been enlightened by Christ. He (she) is to walk always as a child of the light. May he (she) keep the flame of faith alive in his (her) heart. When the Lord comes, may he (she) go out to meet him with all the saints in the heavenly kingdom."[2]

The rite reinforces the understanding of faith as a gift which comes from Christ but which then has to be nurtured and tended by others—godparents, parents, and ultimately the child as he or she matures. The liturgy enables us to visualize the Church's belief and to see it expressed in symbols and gestures.

---

2 Rite of Baptism, *The Catholic Liturgical Library*, accessed July 5, 2017, http://www.catholicliturgy.com/index.cfm/fuseaction/textcontents/index/4/subindex/67/textindex/7.

Baptism is not simply a ritual profession of faith already held—it truly transmits faith through the working of the Holy Spirit. In an adult catechumen, this means sealing, strengthening, and "sacramentalizing" a faith already present and awakened through the process of conversion and the handing on of faith through catechetical formation such as takes place in the Rite of Christian Initiation (RCIA). An infant is unable to freely accept and assent to the faith professed on the child's behalf by godparents and parents as well as the Church as a whole. This underscores the responsibility of the Church and the family to nurture the gift of faith in these young Christians. As Pope Francis explains:

> The structure of baptism, its form as a rebirth in which we receive a new name and a new life, helps us to appreciate the meaning and importance of infant baptism. Children are not capable of accepting the faith by a free act, nor are they yet able to profess that faith on their own; therefore the faith is professed by their parents and godparents in their name.
>
> Since faith is a reality lived within the community of the Church, part of a common "We," children can be supported by others, their parents and godparents, and welcomed into their faith, which is the faith of the Church; this is symbolized by the candle which the child's father lights from the paschal candle.
>
> The structure of baptism, then, demonstrates the critical importance of cooperation between Church and family in passing on the faith. Parents are called, as Saint Augustine once said, not only to bring children

> into the world but also to bring them to God, so that through baptism they can be reborn as children of God and receive the gift of faith.[3]

If faith can be understood as a flame, then it is equally a light. Indeed, this symbolism is rooted in the Easter vigil liturgy in which the Easter fire of Christ's rising first ignites the paschal candle and then is passed person to person through the congregation, dispelling the darkness of confusion, error, and fear. As light, faith can be understood in a twofold way. It is the light and power to respond to God's revelation of himself (which theologians have called the *fides qua*—the "faith by which" we believe) and it is the content of that belief revealed by God in Scripture and tradition and handed on by the Church (the *fides quae*—the "faith which" we believe).[4] When we profess our faith by declaring the creed during the liturgy, we are making an act of faith in both of these senses. Faith is both the content of what we profess (i.e., the articles of the creed) and the light and power by which we believe them to be true (which is the effect of the Holy Spirit living and working in us through the virtue of faith).

Much of the rest of this book will deal with ways in which parents can communicate the content of the faith to their children (the "faith which" we believe)—and we will share some of our own experience of doing so in our family. But how, as parents, do we nurture or stir up in our children

---

3 *Lumen Fidei*, no. 43.

4 See, for example, the treatment offered by William Mattison, *Introducing Moral Theology: True Happiness and the* Virtues (Grand Rapids: Brazos, 2008), 221–27.

the "faith by which" we believe? After all, in this aspect of faith we especially see its dependence on God's grace. We do not create faith in our children nor can we deepen it by our efforts or initiative. It is an infused supernatural habit created, sustained, and deepened by the work of the Holy Spirit. This is a theological question with a host of real-life implications for parents trying to raise their children in the faith, as the Church calls us to do.

If faith is born of the encounter with Christ, then one of our important tasks as parents is to make it possible for our children to continue to encounter Jesus over the course of their lives. Sacraments, particularly the sacraments of initiation (i.e., Baptism, Eucharist, and Confirmation) are certainly key moments where this occurs, but we must look for others. These can be specific events such as vacation Bible schools, retreats, missions, or youth conferences. However, they also need to be more regular practices such as family prayer both at home and in participating in the Church's liturgical worship or religious education. These regular practices create the opportunity for ongoing—even daily—encounters with Jesus.

Pope Francis has challenged us to a "missionary conversion" within the Church in which we see all of our Christian lives and practices in the key of evangelization.[5] All of the members of the Church are called to be not just followers of Jesus but missionaries who share the Gospel with others. This challenge includes our life together and practices as Christian families. By creating opportunities for our children

---

5 See *Evangelii Gaudium*, nos. 20–49, 119–21.

to encounter Christ, the Holy Spirit has the opportunity to create deeper faith in them.

### Cooperating With Grace

Not long ago, John was at a lunch with a colleague. He mentioned that we were writing a book about raising children in a way that prepared them for their future vocations. The colleague said that even though he and his wife are very active in their parish and in the practice of their faith, only one of their three adult children practices the Christian faith. Of the other two, one sees some positive values in their Christian upbringing while the other is a self-described skeptic. He then asked about our children. John mentioned that we were blessed to have all five of our children trying to live and practice their faith and committed to serving the Church in some form. His response was immediate: "You've got to talk about how you did that in your book."

We've had similar conversations with other friends and acquaintances. We have also met many committed Christians who have a deep personal relationship with the Lord and a flourishing prayer life but whose grown children have abandoned the faith, are indifferent to it, or are openly hostile to Christianity. This is a profound source of suffering for these men and women—parents who in some cases, like St. Monica praying for her rebellious son Augustine, have prayed for years for the conversion or reversion of their children.

When people ask, "How did you do it?", our answer is always, "We didn't do it—the grace of God did." And theologically, that is the truth. As we've seen, it is the Holy Spirit who creates and enlivens faith in believers of all ages—parents and children. Furthermore, we can point to many of our shortcomings, failures, and sins as parents to buttress the claim that at times God's grace worked more in spite of us than because of us. But as John's colleague replied when given that answer, "As parents you must have done some things right to have all of your adult children practicing the faith." And on further reflection, we had to admit that that was true as well. While faith is a gift of grace, we are called to do things to cooperate with and deepen that gift—to "stir it into flame" as St. Paul exhorted Timothy. And as parents, we are called to do this not only in ourselves but in our children.

When we told some of our children about John's conversation with his colleague, one of them suggested that they each write a few short reflections on aspects of our family life that helped them to identify with and grow in their faith. We thought that that was an excellent idea. They would have a much better vantage point from which to evaluate what "worked" for them in our family life and practices. Given that each and every person is different and encounters the Lord in a unique way, it would stand to reason that even children raised in the same family environment would have different experiences of what helped them grow in and embrace the faith. So, in no particular order and with their names omitted, we are turning over the rest of this chapter to our children to share some of their thoughts.

***

One summer, our family piled into our Suburban to go on our annual summer vacation. As a teenage boy, the first thing I did was put in my headphones and start listening to music. We had not even gotten on the highway before I was told to turn the music off because we were praying a Rosary as a family. Begrudgingly, I turned off the music to join my family. I knew there was no point in arguing—participating with the family in prayer was not something to be debated.

Growing up in our house, practicing the Catholic faith was not an option but a requirement. Whether it was going to Mass every Sunday, praying before meals, evening prayer as a family, or even a Rosary together in the car, these things were expected. My parents, by their example, ingrained in my siblings and me from our earliest age what it means to be a practicing Catholic. So much so that practicing the faith became habitual for us. It got to the point where some of my siblings would get upset if we opened any presents on Christmas before first saying Christmas morning prayer as a family.

When I moved away from home, I no longer had my parent's example or the requirement to practice my faith. What really cemented these habits I had developed was learning the reason behind all of them. I attended the Catholic University of America where I took many classes in philosophy and theology. This deeper study of the theology of Catholicism and the philosophy of God helped to justify all of the practices and habits I had learned about and been engaged in from a young age. The faith which my parents had helped to foster was now solidified and given life through my own reason and understanding.

As I grew in my journey of uncovering the profound mystery and reality of my Catholic faith, I came to understand that my entire life would be intertwined with and strengthened by it. My wife and I met in college at Catholic University and together we continue to strengthen our shared faith through the sacraments and in the ordinary opportunities of daily life. We work together, with the grace of the Holy Spirit, to set the example our parents did for us, rooting each member of our own growing family in faith. Though our three children are still too young to fully participate and understand, the first thing we do when going on a long car trip is pray a Rosary as a family.

***

When I was in second grade, my Catholic elementary school and the Catholic community attached to it participated in a charismatic retreat. During the evening, we gathered in the school gym to be prayed over. Teams made up of two retreat leaders would circle around the person they were going to pray with, one of them standing in front to pray and the other waiting behind to catch the retreatant if she fell down, "slain in the spirit." When it was my turn, I remember seeing parents, classmates, and their families lying on the floor around me and being torn between stubbornly daring the Holy Spirit to knock me over and just falling backward like everyone else in the gym. In the end, peer pressure won. As I lay on the gym floor, I wondered how long I had to stay there before it would be acceptable to get up and how many other people had fallen backward not out of an overwhelming encounter with the Holy Spirit but because it seemed the thing to do.

The majority of my classmates from that school have not remained practicing Catholics, and as evidence that my inner cynic has not diminished since elementary school, I've occasionally wondered if that retreat is part of the reason why. However, while it and my other experiences as part of that community convinced me that charismatic styles of prayer and liturgy did not appeal to or move me, it did not shake my faith. I think the other aspects of my family's practice of our Catholic faith are the reason for that.

My parents attended the Franciscan University of Steubenville during the height of the charismatic renewal and then participated in the charismatic community of my elementary school when we moved to Maryland. Nevertheless, the type of praise-and-worship centered prayer designed to elicit emotions, which characterizes charismatic prayer, was only part of our family's religious practice. We also regularly incorporated more traditional forms of prayer into our routine, such as the Rosary, novenas (I can still recite the novena to Saint Jude from memory having learned it when we were trying to sell our house when I was fourteen), chaplets, the examination of conscience, Eucharistic adoration, Bible reading, learning about the saints, and regular morning and night prayer as a family. Sacramentals also made a regular appearance in our family life. We used holy water to bless our advent wreath every winter and holy oil to bless us after bad dreams or when we were worried, sad, or scared.

Icons and religious paintings adorned the walls of our home. These are all still part of our religious practice, even now when my siblings and I are grown with our own homes.

Practicing our faith in this way had two important effects on me. First, it demonstrated the "big tent" of Catholicism—there are many modes of prayer and avenues to a relationship with God. As long as they are rooted in the Church's dogma and the sacraments, they are equally valid. So I turned from my discomfort with charismatic prayer and found Gregorian chant, the Divine Office, and other forms of devotion rooted in ancient and medieval practice that I related to more readily

The second, and I think more important, effect of the diversity of our religious practice was that it taught me that faith was not a feeling but an action. While there is a difference between saying the Rosary while deeply meditating on the mysteries as opposed to hurriedly saying the prayers by rote as your mind dwells on other things, prayer is the act of saying the words, regardless of how moved you are each time.

This lesson, combined with our at-home religious education which emphasized a rational approach to faith, provided me with guidance on how to follow the model of faith set forth by Bernard of Clairvaux in the opening of *Fides et Ratio*: "Faith and reason are like two wings on which the human spirit rises to the contemplation of truth." I could see this model at work in my family when, during high school, we read and discussed the *Catechism of the Catholic Church* point by point. I learned that thinking about and assenting to the tenets of faith and performing the work of prayer is what the Christian faith is all about; it frequently has little to do with feelings.

As I grew up, this understanding became increasingly important in my life. In my early twenties, I was diagnosed with depression and an anxiety disorder. As I learned not to always trust my emotions, I was intensely grateful that my upbringing in and experience of Catholicism was not rooted in feelings. When I was unable to find my own words to pray or articulate how I felt, I had a cache of prayers at my disposal, given to me by the Church. And my introduction to the saints through our family's devotion and instruction let me know that I was not alone in feeling this way. Saint John of the Cross, Saint Thérèse of Lisieux, and Saint Teresa of Calcutta all wrote about their own dark nights of the soul, which gave me comfort as well as aspirational models of holiness during this time.

In Catholicism, you are not alone in your attempt to get to heaven. As the Body of Christ, individuals are united to other members of the Church on earth, as well as those in purgatory and in heaven. We have the models of the lives of the saints, a 2,000-plus years library of Catholic theology wrestling with every aspect of and charge against the faith, and myriad prayers and traditions demonstrating the sacredness of ordinary life in addition to the awesome gift of grace from the sacraments. Even growing up, our family's practice of our faith was not a solitary endeavor. It was something we did together.

***

My first year of college was the first time in my life my faith was significantly challenged. However, because of the strong foundation I received from my family growing up, these challenges served as means to build my personal relationship with God rather than break it. Through my childhood and high school years, I never questioned the truth of Catholic teaching. I believe a major reason for this is that my parents made faith the central element of our family's life around which other things revolved rather than just an event we attended on Sundays. We did night prayer as a family most nights and would always begin long car rides by praying the Rosary. Holidays were centered around religious liturgies, and whenever we were traveling or going on vacation, the trip planning would involve finding a Mass in the area. Additionally, seeing all of my siblings remain practicing Catholics reinforced my certainty in being Catholic. These things helped me to know that my faith was true and of central importance to a good life.

When I went to high school, although I knew the importance of my faith, I did not consistently prioritize it, and as a result, I did not always feel a strong connection to God, or even a strong inclination to strengthen that connection. For my last two years of high school, I served as a peer minister for the confirmation candidates at my parish because my friends wanted to but not because I hoped or believed it would contribute to my spiritual development. After retreats with this youth group, I felt a strong desire to grow in my faith, but after time, this feeling faded as I became distracted by school, friends, and sports and sought to find my happiness primarily in these things.

As a result, when I went to college, I did not have a strong personal prayer life that influenced my daily thoughts and actions. I went to Mass every Sunday and learned deeper truths about my faith in my philosophy and theology classes. However, at the same time, I went out to parties every weekend with my friends. The foundation I received from my family along with the truth I was learning in my courses directly contradicted this other part of my lifestyle and actions. As a result, I often felt unhappy and stressed. I learned in my classes that habitual action changes a person's character—who they are. This knowledge along with the example my parents portrayed of living with Christ as the center of one's actions, helped me to realize I needed to form my own life and actions around my faith. Making changes such as no longer going out on weekends and of going to daily Mass several times a week have made a significant difference in decreasing my stress and feelings of unhappiness. I still struggle to form my life and actions around my faith; however, from the foundation of faith I received from my family that is reinforced by the truth I have begun to learn through the study of philosophy and by my own experiences, I have come to desire to more closely align my actions with God's will.

***

Two thoughts come to mind in considering how our parents helped to foster the faith within us as we were growing up while recognizing the work of grace. Our parents taught us to try to understand our faith, not simply to believe it. And faith was not just something we practiced on Sundays.

Our parents helped the faith take root within us by intertwining faith with reason—by allowing and encouraging us to try to understand what we believed. They would not, for example, teach us that we believe in the divinity of Christ simply because we believe it; rather, they would explain that we believe in Christ's divinity and that belief is rational for these reasons. Naturally, these explanations would be in keeping with our age. Words like *nature* and *person* were likely thrown around, but probably not *hypostatic* or *dyothelitism*. And we definitely grew into understanding. For instance, a family story has one of my siblings, in explaining the immateriality of angels, boldly proclaiming that of course they do not have bodies, "they're heads with wings." The key was that, in presenting a tenet of the faith, our parents would try to explain how it made sense, encourage us to think it through, and ask questions. We were never taught to just blindly believe.

This did not mean, however, that our parents discounted the deep mystery and beauty of the faith. They recognized it and would readily present that mystery to us as something that first required an assent of faith. Then we could attempt to understand. Our father, as a theologian, was especially adept in facilitating our understanding, but his knowledge was a helpful, rather than necessary, condition for this. By being taught to use reason in conjunction with faith, we were able to develop a deeper and richer faith. In the words of Saint John Paul II, "Faith and reason are like two wings upon which the human spirit rises to the contemplation of truth."[6]

Our parents also helped to foster the faith within us, making it real and concrete, by never having faith be something we just practiced on Sundays. Faith was an "all week thing," "a daily thing," and both of our parents set an example by prayer and action. They emphasized the need to pray together as a family, resulting in regular night prayer, as well as the somewhat frequent Rosary. They also lived in accordance with the faith, making sure they were not telling us to believe something while contradicting the implications of that belief by their actions. They witnessed to the need to turn to God daily in prayer.

Our mother was striking in this. She would pray for everything—little things, like asking St. Anthony to intercede for us when we lost something, and big things, like God's blessing in selling our house. Her posture was never one of independence and self-sufficiency but rather of an implicit recognition of utter dependence on God in the everyday circumstances of life. By not relegating faith to Sunday alone, but by demonstrating it daily, our parents helped to make faith central in our lives. In Pope Benedict XVI's words, "Our relationship to God should not be confined to such momentary situations, but should be present as the bedrock of our soul."[7]

---

6 Saint John Paul II, encyclical *Fides et Ratio*, no. 1.

7 Pope Benedict XVI, *Jesus of Nazareth: From the Baptism in the Jordan to the Transfiguration*, trans. Adrian Walker (San Francisco: Ignatius, 2008), p. 129.

In short, the answer to how our parents helped the faith take root in us, their children, is that they themselves possessed the faith in its richness, as a faith to be understood and a faith to be lived, and they gave witness to the need for us to do the same.

***

So many of my childhood memories related to my faith are filled with joy. In part, this is because all of the little things my parents did to make these times special, like letting us have a sip of their coffee when we gathered to pray as a family on weekend mornings, or taking us out for donuts after Mass on Sunday. Integrating these little traditions into the practice of our Catholic faith helped to make these times I looked forward to and formed the association that time we set aside for God is unique and something we collectively celebrated.

These traditions also helped me begin to appreciate the beauty and the mystery within Catholicism. One of my favorite times of year were the weeks leading up to Christmas when, each night before dinner, we'd light the candles on the Advent wreath. From an early age, this simple ritual helped me understand that there was something truly magical about Christmas. I'd listen with a sense of wonder and openness to the Bible passage my dad would read each evening to accompany the candle lighting.

These traditions helped captivate my young mind and make Catholicism something I found very appealing and enjoyed practicing. The faith took root in me in a substantial way, however, because these traditions were accompanied by continual learning about what the Church teaches and the reasoning behind that teaching. My parents taught our religious education classes at home, beginning in early elementary school. Around the time I was confirmed, my dad began going through the *Catechism of the Catholic Church* with me. This opportunity to discuss and debate different points until I understood why the Church believed these things increased my appreciation for the depth and beauty of Catholic teaching and made this something I chose to believe for myself. The sense of wonder inspired by elements of Catholicism, such as the Incarnation, deepened as I came to appreciate the logic and immense gift simultaneously present in the Church's theology.

Without the inviting and celebratory approach to the practice of our faith that my parents brought to our family life, I don't know that I would have had the same openness toward or interest in the Gospel. Without their work to reinforce and deepen my understanding of Catholic doctrine, it's likely I would have outgrown my faith and not continued practicing it into adulthood. However, together these have contributed to a faith that allows me to appreciate the inherent wonder in so many of the Church's teachings, to understand and participate in the sacramental ritual of the Mass, and to find the truth that sets us free.

### Key Points

- Faith is born of the encounter with Christ.
- A key task of Christian parents is to create opportunities

for this encounter both in specific events and regular practices which are part of family life.

- The sacraments of initiation are foundational for the Christian life.
- Faith is a gift of grace, yet it can be fostered and developed by our actions and practices.
- Because children are unique persons, the way in which faith takes root in them can be very different even within the same family.

5

# Vocation

The word *vocation* comes from the Latin verb *vocare,* "to call." Therefore, a vocation is a call received from God. Simply by virtue of being baptized into Christ and having the Holy Spirit operative in our lives, every Christian is called to mature and grow in faith, hope, and love. That is, every Christian is called to holiness.

This has been the understanding of the Church from its beginning. Speaking specifically of life in Christian households, the letter to the Hebrews exhorts, "Let mutual love continue. Do not neglect hospitality, for through it some have unknowingly entertained angels. Be mindful of prisoners as if sharing their imprisonment, and of the ill-treated as of yourselves, for you also are in the body. Let marriage be honored among all and the marriage bed be kept undefiled, for God will judge the immoral and adulterers. Let your life be free from love of money but be content with what you have, for he has said, 'I will never forsake you or abandon you'" (Heb 13:1–5).

Married Christians are not called to abandon the world in their pursuit of holiness but to give witness to it through their concrete practice of virtues, such as generosity, charity, chastity, and simplicity in living their daily lives.

After his own conversion, St. John Chrysostom desired to withdraw from the world by embracing a monastic life in the solitude and silence of the desert. He thought that marriage and life in the world were obstacles to the pursuit of holiness. His health, however, proved unsuited to desert life and he had to return to the city. In Antioch, he was ordained a priest and made preacher of the cathedral. He later served as bishop of Constantinople. During these years, St. John's pastoral experience working with families seems to have transformed his view of the possibilities for holiness within marriage and the demands of family life.[1] In one of his homilies, he told the married couples in his congregation:

> Pray together at home and go to Church; when you come back home, let each ask the other the meaning of the readings and the prayers. If you are overtaken by poverty, remember Peter and Paul, who were more honored than kings and rich men, though they spent their lives in hunger and thirst. Remind one another that nothing in life is to be feared, except offending God. If your marriage is like this your perfection will rival the holiest of monks.[2]

---

1 For more on Saint John's life and this evolution in his understanding see Catherine Roth, "Introduction," in *On Marriage and Family Life*, pp. 7–24.

2 St. John Chrysostom, *Homily 20 on Ephesians* in *On Marriage and Family Life,* pp. 61–62.

This is a remarkable statement when we compare it to his early views which suggest that marriage necessarily constituted an obstacle to the pursuit of holiness.

With the growth of monasticism in the fourth and fifth centuries and beyond in both the Eastern and Western Church, many people adopted something like St. John's early views instead of his mature position. Marriage and family life were seen as a kind of lesser option compared to monastic or religious life—a "B team" within the Church in regard to the pursuit of holiness. Monastic or religious life was regarded as a kind of "white martyrdom," closer to the supreme witness of giving one's life for Christ (i.e., "red martyrdom") than a life lived in the world. This two-tiered view of the Christian life colored many people's perception over the centuries, even though there were always voices reminding people that all Christians are called to sanctity. Those voices include such saints as St. Francis De Sales in the sixteenth century or St. Thérèse of Lisieux in the nineteenth.

At the Second Vatican Council (1962–65), the assembled bishops forcefully reminded the Church of the universal call to holiness. In the Dogmatic Constitution on the Church the Council Fathers teach:

> Thus it is evident to everyone, that all the faithful of Christ of whatever rank or status, are called to the fullness of the Christian life and to the perfection of charity. . . . In order that the faithful may reach this perfection, they must use their strength accordingly as they have received it, as a gift from Christ. They must follow in His footsteps and conform themselves to His

> image seeking the will of the Father in all things. They must devote themselves with all their being to the glory of God and the service of their neighbor.
>
> In this way, the holiness of the People of God will grow into an abundant harvest of good, as is admirably shown by the life of so many saints in Church history. The classes and duties of life are many, but holiness is one—that sanctity which is cultivated by all who are moved by the Spirit of God, and who obey the voice of the Father and worship God the Father in spirit and in truth.[3]

So the primary vocation—or call—of all Christians is to become holy in whatever state in life they live.

## Vocation and Vocations

When we give talks, classes, or retreats, we have been amazed to encounter Catholic college students and young adults who have been told that they do not have a vocation—until they enter the priesthood, religious life, or marriage. This is false and even dangerous teaching. Every Christian, joined to Christ in baptism, is called by God to a life of holiness. This is the basic and indelible vocation of every believer. However, this fundamental vocation can be further specified by a call to a particular state of life such as marriage or consecrated life.

When one receives this further call to a state in life, it does not erase the fundamental call to holiness—it further

3 *Lumen Gentium*, nos. 40–41.

concretizes it. In other words, married people become holy by loving their spouse and learning what it means to lay down their life for that person (cf. Eph 5:25–29). Parents becomes holy by caring for their children and forming them in the faith. Pope Francis describes this reality well in one of his catecheses on the family. The quote is lengthy, but it is worth hearing the whole of the Holy Father's teaching on this point:

> All this makes us understand that, in order to be saints, there is no need to be bishops, priests or religious: no, we are all called to be saints! So, many times we are tempted to think that sainthood is reserved only to those who have the opportunity to break away from daily affairs in order to dedicate themselves exclusively to prayer. But it is not so! Some think that sanctity is to close your eyes and to look like a holy icon. No! This is not sanctity!
>
> Sanctity is something greater, deeper, which God gives us. Indeed, it is precisely in living with love and offering one's own Christian witness in everyday affairs that we are called to become saints. And each in the conditions and the state of life in which he or she finds him or herself. But you are consecrated. Are you consecrated? — Be a saint by living out your donation and your ministry with joy. Are you married? — Be a saint by loving and taking care of your husband or your wife, as Christ did for the Church. Are you an unmarried baptized person? — Be a saint by carrying out your work with honesty and competence and

> by offering time in the service of your brothers and sisters. "But, father, I work in a factory; I work as an accountant, only with numbers; you can't be a saint there. . .". "Yes, yes you can! There, where you work, you can become a saint. God gives you the grace to become holy. God communicates himself to you".
>
> Always, in every place, one can become a saint, that is, one can open oneself up to this grace, which works inside us and leads us to holiness. Are you a parent or a grandparent? — Be a saint by passionately teaching your children or grandchildren to know and to follow Jesus. And it takes so much patience to do this: to be a good parent, a good grandfather, a good mother, a good grandmother; it takes so much patience and with this patience comes holiness: by exercising patience. Are you a catechist, an educator or a volunteer? Be a saint by becoming a visible sign of God's love and of his presence alongside us.
>
> This is it: every state of life leads to holiness, always! In your home, on the street, at work, at church, in that moment and in your state of life, the path to sainthood has been opened. Don't be discouraged to pursue this path. It is God alone who gives us the grace. The Lord asks only this: that we be in communion with Him and at the service of our brothers and sisters.[4]

As parents, our goal is to raise our children to be saints. If we lead them to the Lord and work to foster their relationship

---

4 Weekly General Audience, November 19, 2014.

with him, they will be able to hear God's call to them and enter the state of life he desires for them. But above all, they will hear God's call to them to live a life of holiness.

### A Few Theological Qualifications on Vocation

In order to prevent misunderstandings, a few important points should be appended to this discussion. First, God calls us because he loves us—not because we deserve it or are somehow worthy. A recurring theme in Scripture is that when someone is called by God, their immediate response is to protest because of their sinfulness or limitations. Moses protests that he does not speak well (Ex 4:10–16), while Jeremiah says he is too young (Jer 1:6–8). Isaiah and Simon Peter are immediately aware of their sinfulness and fearful of remaining in the divine presence (Is 6:5–7; Lk 5:8–10). These protests point to a basic truth. We are finite and sinful beings; God calls us in spite of these realities. Saint Paul states it directly: "God proves his love for us in that while we were still sinners Christ died for us" (Rom 5:8). Lives of holiness, like those we see in the saints, are the fruit of a generous response to God's gracious love and mercy over time. We are not born saints.[5]

Second, while the Church has always called its members to holiness, this does not mean that she has viewed all states in life as equivalent or interchangeable. Based on the witness of Jesus himself, St. John the Baptist, and St. Paul (as

---

[5] Even the Blessed Mother, whom we honor as the queen of the saints, was preserved from original sin in view of the future redemption achieved by her Divine Son—not by any merit of her own.

well as Paul's explicit teaching; cf. 1 Cor 7:7–9, 25–40), the Church has always taught the superiority of celibacy for the sake of the kingdom to marriage. In the early fifth century, Saint Augustine used the analogy of Martha and Mary (cf. Lk 10:38–42) to make the point. Marriage is good—we see this by analogy in Martha who was busy with the details of hospitality and life in the world. Virginity is better—we see this by analogy in Mary who was focused on listening to the Lord and his word.[6]

But what does it mean to say that one state in life is higher or superior to another? St. John Paul II insisted that, rightly understood, the objective superiority of consecrated virginity does not devalue marriage: "That *'superiority' of continence over marriage never means, in the authentic Tradition of the Church, a devaluation of marriage* or an impairment of its essential value."[7] For John Paul II, celibacy is higher in what it signifies—the spousal union of Christ and the Church and the wedding feast of heaven. Marriage signifies these realities mediately—sacramentalizing them in the persons of the Christian couple. This teaching in no way indicates that celibates are better Christians or holier than those called to marriage or living as single persons.

Third, having said all of this, can we speak of priesthood, religious life, or marriage as vocations? Yes, they can be understood as "calls within a call." In these further callings, the basic baptismal summons God gives to every Christian is directed for its realization to a specific path, with specific

---

6 See *On the Good of Marriage*, ch. 8.

7 Weekly General Audience of April 7, 1982 (our translation).

persons. The diversity of states of life within the Church, like the many gifts which God gives, contributes to the flourishing of the Body of Christ as a whole (cf. 1 Cor 12, 14). The amazing thing is that though the call to holiness is given to every Christian and the call to specific states in life are given to large numbers of believers, they are heard in utterly unique ways by those who receive them. God's call to holiness to each Christian is as unique as each person to whom it is given. The call to priesthood, consecrated life, or marriage is also given and received in a unique way by those who hear it.

Fourth and finally, there are people who believe that there is only one person in the world created for them to marry. Certainly, God in his infinite wisdom and knowledge knows who it is that we will choose to marry—though his foreknowledge never overrides our freedom. But the idea can become problematic if we understand it to mean that there is only one person with whom one can be happily and successfully married. Our culture sometimes creates exaggerated romantic ideals of a "soulmate" with whom someone is perfectly matched. This can feed into our current culture of divorce when problems and challenges arise in a marriage as they always do. People assume that the person to whom they are married cannot be their soulmate since they are having problems, and so they have to look elsewhere. The truth is that once two people commit themselves to each other in marriage, God wills for their marriage to flourish and gives them the grace they need to live out their vocation together.

And people can always learn and develop the skills that they need to improve their marriages.[8]

### Our Two Calls to One Another

*Claire*

I think back to when I was a little girl and remember so vividly how much I loved my mom and dad. I knew that they loved me and would do anything for me. I was especially close to my mother and knew from the beginning (or at least from around five years old) that I wanted to be a wife and mother just like her. This was always my heart's desire. I even took time in my college years to discern if this was really God's plan for my life or if he was calling me to the single or religious life. After much prayer, I felt confirmed that God was calling me to the married life and rejoiced that I would someday be a wife and mother.

I was also grateful to my parents for their witness of a loving marriage and what it means to live out the sacrament of marriage. It wasn't until I took a sacraments class in college that I began to understand more deeply what a great gift God has given us in providing channels of his grace in the sacraments. This gave me the language and framework to understand what I saw lived out in my parents' life together.

It was my mother who taught me the importance of prayer in my life and helped me to develop a prayer life and

---

8 On this see John and Claire Grabowski, *One Body: A Program of Marriage Preparation and Enrichment for the New Evangelization* (Steubenville, OH: Emmaus Road Press, 2018), chapters 11 and 12.

a personal relationship with the Lord. She brought me with her to her Bible studies and prayer meetings and I joined her in praying the Rosary and the Divine Mercy Chaplet. She taught me to know that God loved me and had a great plan for my life. I also learned to trust in God to take care of me and to guide me as I prayed and listened to him.

My mom always prayed for me—this is one of the most important things she did for me. She frequently asked the Lord to send me a husband who would treat me like a precious gem—a man who loved the Lord and would show this love in the way he loved me. I am grateful for this prayer of my mother's. I know that God answered her prayer as he worked in John's life, preparing him to be my husband. Later I learned John's mother did not expect to have another child when she conceived him. She was forty-four years old, had had one of her ovaries removed, and was a smoker. I also discovered that my mom had German measles when she was pregnant with me, and yet God protected me from the disease and its effects. I was reminded of the Scripture passage that says that God knew us before we were born and knit us in our mother's womb (cf. Ps 139:13; Jer 1:5). God had a plan for our lives and our life together.

Now I have three daughters and two sons for whom I have been praying since they were born. We pray every day that God will guide them to know his great plan for their lives and to help them to follow that plan. Since their birth, I have prayed for their future spouses, if it's God's will for them to marry. I pray that that he will bring my daughters men who will treat them as precious gems, that my sons will love their wives in that same way, and that our son's wives will love and respect them as men of God. It is never too early to start praying for our children's spouses.

### *John*

I had a conversion experience while in high school and became involved in a local youth group. One of the things which the group did was to attend youth conferences at the University of Steubenville. While there, I learned about the school and its faith environment, and I became interested in studying there. This was confirmed by a "Come and See" weekend visit during my senior year—a weekend at which I met and became friends with a girl named Claire from Long Island. I did not enter college with a clear idea of what I wanted to study or what I would do as a career. I decided to major in theology because I knew that I wanted to serve the Church in some fashion and this seemed a way in which to be trained in order to do it. What exactly I might do with a bachelor's degree in theology did not weigh heavily in my deliberation.

Freshman year was a whirlwind. Claire and I resumed our friendship and had begun dating by October. Like many first-year college students, I found myself overextended between a heavy course load and a host of extracurricular activities. I signed up for a variety of different ministries on and off of campus and found myself feeling over-committed and beginning to burn out. I took the matter to prayer and felt that the Lord showed me that my problem was that whenever I saw needs on campus, I presumed that it was my job to fill them. Rather, all I needed to do was what he called me to do—I did not have to save the world. If everyone on the campus did that, all of the needs would be met and no one would be overextended. It was an important lesson which I have had to learn over and over again during the years since then.

We continued to date into our sophomore year, but as I tried to think and pray about the long-term prospects for our relationship, I ran into a kind of road block. I had a nagging idea that God might be calling me to the priesthood. I felt that I could not continue to date Claire with this question unresolved. I told her that we needed to stop dating for a period of time while I discerned this. I'm not sure that she fully understood, and I know that many of her friends did not (and saw me as the biggest jerk on campus), but I felt like our relationship generated too much emotional static for me to be able to pray and discern clearly. Besides, it did not seem fair to her to continue our dating relationship if I was not certain that I was ultimately called to marriage. So for one semester, we stopped dating, though we did our best to remain friends and support one another.

It was while praying one day during this period that the Lord reminded me of what he had shown me the previous year. I realized that my conflict was due to my looking at the Church and seeing the need for more men to enter the priesthood and presuming that I had to meet this need. Once again, the Lord reminded me that all I had to do was what he called me to do. If everyone in the Church did this, all of the needs in the Body of Christ would be met. Once I saw this, it became very clear to me that God was calling me to marriage and I did not have to be conflicted about my love for Claire. We resumed dating, were engaged at the beginning of our senior year, and were married two weeks before our graduation—that way, our friends were able to travel from Steubenville to Long Island for the wedding before dispersing for the summer vacation.

In our thirty-three years of marriage, we have had times of great joy and times of suffering and trial, but I have never doubted that it was God's call to us. I am grateful to have chosen a spouse whose personality and gifts are very different from mine and yet who challenges and complements me in a host of ways. The author of Proverbs puts it well: "Home and possessions are an inheritance from parents, but a prudent wife is from the LORD" (Prv 19:14).

## Key Points

- The word *vocation* means "call."
- All Christians have a baptismal vocation to grow in holiness as followers of Jesus.
- This basic vocation is then further specified by a "call within a call" to a particular state of life (e.g., marriage, religious celibacy, priesthood).
- While there is not only one "soulmate" with whom people can find happiness, married couples can understand themselves as having been called together by God.

6

# Teaching by Word and Example

Realizing that marriage is indeed a vocation, a calling from God, challenges the way we think about and prepare for it. John has had the privilege of teaching seminarians and men and women religious at the Catholic University of America for some twenty-seven years. Those preparing for ordination or religious life typically spend many years in formation studying philosophy, theology, and pastoral practice while at the same time undergoing intensive personal and spiritual formation. Marriage is also a lifelong vocation, yet most marriage preparation programs consist of six or seven sessions or perhaps a weekend retreat. The contrast could not be more glaring. Ignoring this discrepancy—especially in an increasingly confused and anti-marriage culture—is a recipe for disaster and undoubtedly contributes to the scourge of divorce which affects so many Christian families.

To address this issue, the Church's pastors have increasingly turned their attention to the family as a place of formation. Pope St. John Paul II, in his 1981 apostolic exhortation *Familiaris Consortio*, identified three stages of preparation for the vocation of marriage—remote, proximate, and immediate.[1]

---

[1] See *Familiaris Consortio*, no. 66.

Remote preparation begins in early childhood as children are formed in basic truths of the Christian faith: the reality of God, creation, the fall of humanity, salvation through Jesus, the sending of the Holy Spirit, and the gift of the Church. They are also formed in fundamental human values such as the dignity of human persons made in God's image, the nature of love, the reality of good and evil, the need for forgiveness, the nature of truth, and the goodness of the body with its inherent sexual differentiation. This twofold foundation in Christian faith and moral values prepares children for later making a gift of themselves in love, whether in marriage or in priesthood or consecrated religious life.

Proximate preparation for marriage also takes place under the oversight of the parents, though they typically share this responsibility for forming their children with religious educators in the Church. This involves forming school age children and usually occurs in the context of preparing them for the sacraments of Penance, Eucharist, and Confirmation. This stage entails a deeper formation in Christian morality, including providing a deeper understanding of sexuality, marriage, and family life. This instruction should take place in cooperation with the parents and in an age-appropriate manner, providing a basis for young people to discern God's call regarding their future state of life.[2]

Further formation for a future vocation typically takes place outside of the home and family. Immediate preparation aims

---

2 An excellent overview of such age-appropriate formation in human sexuality as ordered to marriage is provided by the 1996 document of the Pontifical Council for the Family *The Truth and Meaning of Human Sexuality.*

to equip couples who are engaged to be married with vital information in advance of their wedding. This is what most people think of when they think of marriage preparation or formation. In recent years, the Church has increasingly drawn attention to the need for ongoing accompaniment and formation of couples *beyond* the wedding.[3] Thus Pope Francis notes, "It is all the more essential that couples be helped during the first years of their married life to enrich and deepen their conscious and free decision to have, hold and love one another for life. Often the engagement period is not long enough, the decision is precipitated for various reasons and, what is even more problematic, the couple themselves are insufficiently mature. As a result, the newly married couple need to complete a process that should have taken place during their engagement."[4]

We have done immediate preparation of engaged couples for marriage for around twenty-five years. For the last nine years, we have been involved in a "post-Cana" marriage ministry for those in our parish who are already married. As important as these moments are in forming Christian couples, they are not our focus in this work.[5] Instead, our focus is on the formation that happens within the family—remote and proximate preparation, to use St. John Paul II's terms. This means thinking about the role of parents as teachers of their children.

---

3 See, for example, Pope John Paul II, *Familiaris Consortio*, no. 69; and Pope Francis, *Amoris Laetitia,* nos. 217–30.

4 *Amoris Laetitia*, no. 217.

5 For a program of formation which can be used for immediate formation (pre-Cana) or ongoing formation of those already married, see our work *"And the Two Shall Become One Body."*

## Mothers and Fathers as Teachers

The rite of Baptism highlights the role of parents as teachers of the faith. After praying a blessing specifically for the mother, the celebrant prays a blessing for the parents, interceding for them in their teaching ministry: "God is the giver of all life, human and divine. May he bless the father of this child. He and his wife will be the first teachers of their child in the ways of faith. May they be also the best of teachers, bearing witness to the faith by what they say and do, in Christ Jesus our Lord."[6]

Note that the rite of Baptism acknowledges the teaching role of both parents, even in the context of a blessing for the child's father. This points to the fact that children need the contributions of both parents. Pope Francis has insisted on multiple occasions that children need and have a right to a mother and a father to care for, love, and teach them:

> Every child has a right to receive love from a mother and a father; both are necessary for a child's integral and harmonious development. As the Australian Bishops have observed, each of the spouses "contributes in a distinct way to the upbringing of a child. Respecting a child's dignity means affirming his or her need and natural right to have a mother and a father." We are speaking not simply of the love of father and mother as individuals, but also of their mutual love, perceived

---

6 See the "Blessing" in "The Rite of Baptism," *Catholic Liturgical Library*, accessed July 21, 2017, http://www.catholicliturgy.com/index.cfm/FuseAction/TextContents/Index/4/SubIndex/67/TextIndex/7.

> as the source of one's life and the solid foundation of the family. Without this, a child could become a mere plaything.
>
> Husband and wife, father and mother, both "cooperate with the love of God the Creator, and are, in a certain sense, his interpreters". They show their children the maternal and paternal face of the Lord. Together they teach the value of reciprocity, of respect for differences and of being able to give and take. If for some inevitable reason one parent should be lacking, it is important to compensate for this loss, for the sake of the child's healthy growth to maturity.[7]

One reason why children need the contributions of both parents is that men and women have different gifts which they bring to bear on the common task of teaching their children.

Based on his own observation and his reading of the opening chapters of Genesis, St. John Paul II taught that women's unique role in bringing new life into the world illuminates some of the distinctive gifts of women. Thus he wrote, "The moral and spiritual strength of a woman is joined to her awareness that God entrusts the human being to her in a special way. Of course, God entrusts every human being to each and every other human being. But this entrusting concerns women in a special way—precisely by reason of their

---

7 *Amoris laetitia*, no. 172; see also his address to the International Colloquium on the Complementarity of Man and Woman Sponsored by the Congregation for the Doctrine of the Faith, November 17, 2014.

femininity—and this in a particular way determines their vocation."[8]

Commenting on the unique bonds formed between women and their children in pregnancy, childbirth, and the early nurturing of children discussed in an earlier chapter, he notes, "This unique contact with the new human being developing within her gives rise to an attitude towards human beings—not only towards her own child, but every human being—which profoundly marks the woman's personality. It is commonly thought that women are more capable than men of paying attention to another person, and that motherhood develops this predisposition even more."[9]

In other words, John Paul II taught that women's capacity to nurture and sustain life creates in them an orientation toward persons and a capability to build relationships and foster communion among persons. These gifts are enhanced by motherhood—whether biological or spiritual.

There is a reason why the rite of Baptism mentions the teaching role of parents in the context of a blessing for fathers. One of the distinctive features of fatherhood identified in Scripture is that fathers have an important role in teaching their children. At times, the terms *father* and *teacher* are used interchangeably (cf. Jgs 17:10; 1 Cor 4:14). The Bible describes specific rituals aimed at promoting a father's involvement with his children, based on Israel's experience of Yahweh as a caring, involved, nurturing Father.[10] In biblical

---

8 *Mulieris Dignitatem*, no. 18.

9 Ibid.

10 See the excellent overview provided by John W. Miller, *Calling God Father: Essays on the Bible, Fatherhood, and Culture*, 2nd ed.

times, this would involve teaching his sons a trade, assisting with discipline, and teaching all of his children the truths of their religious faith in the context of family life and religious practice.

Men often find themselves outside of the early bonds formed between their wives and children and may well "learn their fatherhood" from their wives as St. John Paul II observed, but they still have much to teach their children. Contemporary research supports the idea that if women more typically provide a baseline of nurture for children, men often complement this by setting boundaries and promoting healthy risk-taking.[11] They also play a critical role in modeling the faith to their children. Recent studies highlight the powerful impact of a father's witness in practicing the faith on the later religious practice of their children.[12]

Obviously, these are generalizations that will vary to some degree from person to person, couple to couple. Men and women have distinctive vocations (fatherhood and

---

(New York: Paulist Press, 1999).

11 This is supported even by fairly secular neuroscience and psychology. See, for example, Luann Brizendine, *The Male Brain: A Breakthrough Understanding of How Men and Boys Think* (New York: Three Rivers Press, 2010).

12 A study conducted by the Swiss government in 1994 and published in 2000 found that if a father does not go to church—no matter how faithful his wife's attendance—only one child in fifty will become a regular worshipper. If a father does go regularly, regardless of the practice of the mother, between two-thirds and three-quarters of their children will become churchgoers (whether regular or irregular). See Tara K. E. Brelinsky, "Dads Make All the Difference: Keeping Kids Catholic," *Ignited by Truth*, accessed July 24, 2017, https://ignitedbytruth.org/dads-make-all-the-difference-keeping-kids-catholic/.

motherhood) and gifts, but the way these are expressed will be instantiated differently based on differing personalities and the impact of culture. Certainly, women can and do discipline and encourage healthy risk-taking and men do nurture. Rigid assumptions about gender specific roles or "men's or women's work" are ultimately unhelpful in the life of a Christian family. Spouses must learn to work together with their differing gifts and personalities—it takes two to raise and form children well.

### Teaching by Example and Practices

Much of the teaching that takes place in a family is not communicated through words but through the example given by witness and regular practices. Parents, through their actions, model for their children what it means to love and be loved, to forgive others when injured, or to treat others with gentleness or respect. The words of parents teaching about the faith have much more force when children see that they cohere with the way their parents live. And when parents fail—as we all do—children need to see them accept responsibility for their sin and ask forgiveness (even if this means asking forgiveness of the child). This is why Pope Francis frequently encourages couples and families to place simple phrases such as "please," "thank you," and "I'm sorry" at the center of their lives together because these words connect to deeper attitudes and practices at the heart of authentic human and Christian relationships.[13] Using these words points to and

13 See, for example, his words from the window of the archbishop of Krakow during his apostolic journey to Poland, July 28, 2016; cf.

helps to develop virtues such as kindness, generosity, and contrition.

Formation, in the home of a Christian family, is ultimately aimed at creating an environment where its members can grow in virtue and holiness. This refers not just to the theological virtues of faith, hope, and love, but moral virtues such as temperance, chastity, justice, mercy, and prudence. Developing such virtues requires consistent action over time, shaped and sustained by regular practices and a community that encourages them. Occasional good acts are not sufficient. For Christians, the process of ongoing conversion and growth in virtue is not the result of human willpower and effort but a response to the gift of grace and the work of the Holy Spirit in our lives.

Ideally in a Christian family, over time, all of the members help to form one another. Spouses in particular are called to form one another and help each other grow in holiness.[14] When children are young, parents have a special responsibility to form them. However, even at a young age, children can be examples or witnesses to their parents of faith, simplicity, innocence, or sometimes just perspective on life that frees them from whatever adult problem they are stuck in at the moment. It is for this reason that Jesus points to children as models of discipleship or as particularly blessed in the Gospels (cf. Mt 18:1–5; 19:13–15; Mk 10:13–16; Lk 18:15–17).

---

*Amoris Laetitia*, no. 133.

14 Pope Francis teaches that one aim of marriage ministry is to equip spouses for this task of forming each other (see *Amoris Laetitia*, nos. 218, 221).

But especially as children get older, they become more capable of teaching and forming their parents on a consistent basis. We have seen this with our own children as they have grown, and cannot number all of the times they have encouraged, inspired, challenged, or taught us. When children reach adulthood, their relationship with their parents becomes more of a Christian friendship between people of different ages, though still marked by the unique bonds of respect and affection.

The remainder of this book is largely devoted to practices that should characterize the Christian family as a place of mutual formation ordered to the holiness of its members. However, the precondition of all such practices and the requirement for their fruitfulness is for families to learn to prioritize their time in order to be together. Parents can only teach and form their children if they are with them.

### The Gift of Time

When we first got married and started having children, we made a challenging decision together. We decided that in spite of the financial challenges, we did not want to place our kids in day care so that we could both work or go to school. Deciding, at that point, to have Claire be a stay-at-home mom seemed impossible with John a full-time graduate student who could only do outside work (as a janitor in a Catholic hospital) during summers and over the Christmas break. We made a decision to try to put our faith into action and to prioritize seeking God's kingdom for ourselves and our children, trusting that he would supply our needs (see Mt 6:25–24).

And provide for us God did. What seemed humanly impossible, he made possible for us (cf. Mt 19:26). We ended up having three children before John finished his doctorate. When we look back on those years, we are amazed at how God blessed and provided for our family—often in miraculous ways. These ranged from anonymous gifts of money coming in the mail to people bringing us food. We were able to buy our first computer with a check from an anonymous benefactor to Marquette's graduate program. We had a freezer full of beef that friends donated to us when they bought half of a cow for their own family. Claire was able to work odd jobs while John stayed home with the children in the midst of his studies.

As we tried to step out in faith by prioritizing time with our children, we worked to share with them the ways in which God was taking care of us. It was a common practice—whether during night prayer together or during our family dinner—to talk about the miracles of that particular day. Having to trust in God's providence on a daily basis opened our eyes to the incredible ways he supplied our needs. Claire frequently said, during and after that time, that she could write a book describing all of the miraculous ways God provided for us. And given that our children heard about each one not just when it happened but subsequently in remembering and thanking God for his provision, they could have helped to write it as well.

When we do marriage preparation with couples, one thing we do is to relate the importance of "the two tables" at the heart of our family's life—the family dinner table and the table of the Lord at the Eucharist. As we have said, we made sure that we attended Mass as a family every Sunday (or Saturday evening) no matter what else was going on—vacation, kid's sports, family events—it didn't matter. We wanted our children to see the importance of receiving God's grace in the sacraments—especially the Eucharist, which is the very center of our lives as Christians. But in addition to the table of the Lord, we made family dinner each evening another priority. This has been the best time for us to teach (and learn from) our kids by word and example. During dinner, we could share in depth about what God was doing in our lives, or about the particular feast day, or we could discuss the relation between our faith and current events or the books our children were reading.

Preparing family meals was also a chance to spend time together and then to come together to enjoy eating what God had provided for us. We are grateful that to this day all of our children make attending the Eucharist a priority in their lives. They also all love to cook and to enjoy good food. When we are together at holidays or on family vacations, worshipping together at Mass and sharing family dinners still highlight our time together.

Another important decision that we made in order to invest time in our children was to homeschool each of them around their middle school years. Our kids' first years at school were spent at Catholic and public schools as we tried to find a good fit for our kids and our budget. But as our older daughters approached middle school age, we were concerned about our available options. We could not afford to put multiple kids in Catholic school—and had already discovered that even private schools have limitations—and the local public middle schools seemed problematic, both academically and in terms of their social environment. We knew that the middle school years are difficult as kids try to figure out who they are and what they believe. We decided to homeschool during those years in order to give them a stronger academic foundation and also work on our relationships with them as they entered their teenage years. Given that we are both educators, we decided to share the responsibility—with Claire covering math, science, and grammar, and John doing history, writing, and languages (Latin or French). We may not have covered every subject completely when we homeschooled them, but we worked at teaching our children how to learn, how to think well, and how to write clearly. We also shared the responsibility of catechizing them in the faith in addition to enrolling them in faith formation classes at our parish.

Each child was different, and our mantra was "one kid, one year at a time." Our second daughter actually started before middle school (so that she could be at home with her older sister) and went back before high school. One of our sons didn't seem to have the temperament for homeschooling, so we decided against it. After trying public middle school, however, he came home and made a case for himself based on the bad influences he was exposed to even on the school bus. We were impressed with his reasons, and so he did seventh and eighth grades at home (we suspect that being able to sleep later also had something to do with the attraction for him).

All of our kids played sports in various youth leagues and summer camps giving them plenty of interaction and competition with other kids. They all returned to an academically demanding public high school and excelled. But more than the academics, they went in with a strong foundation in their faith and were able to witness to others instead of just following the culture. When our youngest reached middle school age, we seriously considered keeping her in the local middle school. Her siblings, however, protested, "You have to give her what you gave us." Again, we were convinced and impressed. It was clear to us that our children valued the time we had invested in them, so our youngest spent her middle school years at home.

Not everyone has the time or resources to effectively homeschool their children, or the money to afford private schools. At times, both parents have to work to make ends meet. But these parents can still prioritize their children by investing the time which they do have in them. They can help their children with homework, cheer them on at sports events, and volunteer at school and other activities. Even if their children are enrolled in religious education or sacramental preparation programs at their parish, parents retain their responsibility as the primary educators of their children in the faith and must work to fulfill this responsibility.

The precondition of our being able to fulfill our calling and responsibility as parents to teach and form our children through word and example is to find ways to prioritize our time with them. Whether in making decisions about work versus being at home, or in finding regular practices in daily life like attending Mass together or prioritizing family dinners, God abundantly blesses time family members set aside to be with each other. Our experience has been that by being open to God's direction for our lives and taking small steps, God's miraculous provision and gracious generosity far exceeds our halting efforts.

**Key Points**

- Married couples need formation before and after their wedding to live the vocation of marriage.
- Christian parents are the first and primary teachers of their children in the faith.
- Men and women make unique and irreplaceable contributions in the formation of their children.
- This teaching role of parents is carried out through both words and the witness of actions and practices.
- Finding ways to prioritize time with our children is indispensable to being able to live out this teaching role.

7

# Family as Domestic Church, Sanctuary, and Community

The New Testament makes reference to "house churches"—groups of believers who met for prayer and worship in people's homes. For example, we read of early Christian communities that met in the homes of Aquila and Priscilla (1 Cor 16:19; Rom 16:3, 5), of Philemon (Phlm 1:2), and of Nympha in Laodicea (Col 4:15). This is largely due to historical circumstances. The first Christian communities were generally small groups of believers with limited resources, and they were subjected to sporadic bouts of persecution by Roman authorities from the first century to the fourth. However, this biblical usage gave rise to the idea that Christian homes or families were themselves "little churches." After all, Jesus had taught that where two or three of his disciples gathered in his name, he was present in their midst (see Mt 18:20).

Based on this understanding, early Christian teachers developed the idea that the family is an ecclesial reality—a little cell in the Body of Christ. Saint Augustine refers to the Christian family as an *ecclesia domestica* ("a domestic church") and saw this reality lived out through its practices such as prayer, discipleship, and encouraging members to embrace celibacy.[1]

Saint John Chrysostom likewise encourages couples to make their homes a church by focusing on the Scriptures and their role in forming the family:

> Therefore, all these things we should retain, my dear ones, and so we should put in (your) home both altars, one for food and the other for the sacred readings. Indeed, the man should repeat those things which are appointed; the wife, moreover, should learn thoroughly, the children should listen, nor should the servants be defrauded of these readings. Make your home a church. Indeed the salvation (welfare) of both your children and your servants (must be rendered by you).[2]

Saint John Chrysostom sees the liturgy of the Church extending into the practices of the home. We saw above his insistence that the religious practices of the home such as simplicity of life, prayer, and pondering the Scriptures can make married couples as holy as any monks.[3]

---

1 See his *De bono viduitatis* and *Epistolae nuper in lucem prolatae*. For an overview of the idea of domestic church in the New Testament and the Fathers of the Church, see the excellent study by Joseph Atkinson, *The Biblical and Theological Foundations of the Family: The Domestic Church* (Washington, DC: The Catholic University of America Press, 2014).

2 *Shorter Commentary on Genesis*, 7 (*PG* 54:607). The translation is that of Atkinson, *Biblical and Theological Foundations of the Family*, 283.

3 See *Homily 20 on Ephesians*.

Though this idea was present in the Church's first centuries, it fell into disuse for the next one and a half millennia—perhaps because of the focus on monastic and other religious forms of Christian community. The bishops at the Second Vatican Council, however, revived the idea:

> From the wedlock of Christians there comes the family, in which new citizens of human society are born, who by the grace of the Holy Spirit received in baptism are made children of God, thus perpetuating the people of God through the centuries. The family is, so to speak, the domestic church. In it parents should, by their word and example, be the first preachers of the faith to their children; they should encourage them in the vocation which is proper to each of them, fostering with special care vocation to a sacred state.[4]

Echoing this usage, the *Catechism of the Catholic Church* states concisely, "The Christian family constitutes a specific revelation and reflection of ecclesial communion and for this reason can and should be called a domestic church."[5] This idea has featured prominently in the teaching of St. John Paul II and Pope Francis and will be developed in coming chapters, especially the family's participation in Christ's priestly, prophetic, and kingly offices which Pope John Paul II highlighted. However, first it is worth pondering a few other terms which can describe the ecclesial nature of the Christian family.

---

4 Dogmatic Constitution on the Church, *Lumen Gentium*, no. 11.

5 CCC 2204.

## Family as Sanctuary

Recent Church teaching has used other terms to capture the Christian family's role as a living cell in the Body of Christ. St. John Paul II, for example, referred to the family as a "sanctuary of life" integral to building a larger "culture of life": "The family has a special role to play throughout the life of its members, from birth to death. It is truly 'the sanctuary of life: the place in which life—the gift of God—can be properly welcomed and protected against the many attacks to which it is exposed, and can develop in accordance with what constitutes authentic human growth.' Consequently the role of the family in building a culture of life is decisive and irreplaceable."[6]

The idea of family as a sanctuary of life would encompass the couple's mission to generously welcome life discussed in chapter one. It would also include a family's responsibility to care for its elderly, sick, or disabled members as well as other vulnerable members of the community of which it is part—the unborn, the poor, the marginalized, the homeless, or strangers. In all of these ways, families give witness to the preciousness of life as a gift from God.

But the Christian family is a sanctuary in other senses beyond its service to life. The word *sanctuary* comes from the Latin word *sanctuarium* which means a holy place or a shrine. We use it to describe the space around the altar of a church where the Eucharist is celebrated or, by extension, the church building itself. The term can also denote a place of

---

6 *Evangelium Vitae*, no. 92 (citing his earlier encyclical *Centesimus Annus*, no. 39).

refuge or asylum where one can flee from enemies. A Christian family can be thought of as a sanctuary in both of these senses. Certainly, because of the Holy Spirit living within its members, a Christian family is a holy place—a space for the presence of God within the world. It also ought to be a refuge from negative or destructive forces in the world which oppose the family's call to grow in holiness.

It is easy to identify some of the chief threats to living as a Christian family which parents have to strive to keep out of their homes or to counteract when their children are exposed to them in the wider culture—the poison of pornography, attacks on Christian faith or religious freedom, the various forms of moral relativism, ideologies which confuse desires with identities, anti-life or anti-family impulses in the culture, or the scourge of racism. Most Christian parents are alert to these threats and quick to respond when their children encounter them. However, parents may not be aware of how easily some of these threats can invade their homes through the growing number of internet-connected devices.[7]

But there are more subtle threats that can invade the sanctuary of the family and rob Christian families of their joy and their ability to give witness to those around them. These include things like busyness, the materialism of our

---

7 For example, Focus on the Family estimates that the average age of first exposure to pornography in American homes is now eight years old. See Rob Jackson, "When Children View Pornography," Focus on the Family, accessed March 18, 2017, http://www.focusonthefamily.com/parenting/sexuality/when-children-use-pornography/when-children-view-pornography.

consumer culture, technology, and the reach of the media. Setting limits on the presence and reach of these things in our homes and in our children's lives is vital to making our families a sacred space and place of refuge. But it is not enough to "just say no" to certain things; we have to actively work to give our children positive alternatives to capture their minds, hearts, and imaginations with what is genuinely true, good, and beautiful (cf. Phil 4:8).

Technology joined to our consumer culture poses a particular challenge and one that has grown exponentially in recent years. It is ironic that technology, which can join people together from all over the world in text, audio, or video communication, can disconnect people living under the same roof as they retreat from one another into their own smart phones, computers, or other devices. Pope Francis diagnoses the problem in his straightforward fashion:

> Conviviality is a sure barometer for measuring the health of relationships: if in a family something has gone awry, or there is some hidden wound, it is immediately understood at the table. A family that hardly ever eats together, or that does not talk at the table but watches television, or looks at a smartphone, is a "barely familial" family. When children are engrossed with a computer at the table, or a mobile phone, and do not talk to each other, this is not a family, it is like a boarding house."[8]

---

8 Francis, Weekly General Audience, November 11, 2015.

It is important for families to resist this technological disconnect from each other and to prioritize time for real interaction with each other.

### Making Our Home a Sanctuary

One of the rules we had for our children when they were young was that each child could only be involved in one sport or other extracurricular activity at a time. They had to decide what sport or club they wanted to be part of in a given semester or season. If they wanted to try something new, they had to stop the other activity. It worked out well when the boys played the same sport over the years (baseball, football, or ultimate frisbee). As important as sports were to our children, we made sure that Mass and other forms of family time remained a higher priority. If practice or a game interfered with church, we skipped the sport that day. Even when we were away—either on a family vacation or at a sports tournament—we always found a church to go to Mass together. If practices went late into an evening, we would eat late as a family.

Our decision to have Claire be a stay-at-home mom not only enabled her to have time to devote to our family, it also forced us to do without some material things common in families around us. For these reasons, we think that it was one of the best decisions we made together as parents. Claire had time to focus on teaching and forming our children, but we had to live simply as a family. We had one car for the first eighteen years of our marriage—yet another reason to limit kids' activities. We also didn't have most of the gadgets that were invading many other households. We didn't have a video gaming unit in our house until one of our children who had almost finished high school saved enough money to buy a used one for himself. We had only one television and watched it very little, primarily to watch football and indulge our passion for the Green Bay Packers. When our oldest daughter was in high school, a classmate did a survey on the number of televisions people had in their houses. No one could believe that our family only had one. One of the kids asked, "What do you do when everyone wants to watch something different?" Our daughter replied, "You don't."

Like many other parents, we worked to monitor what our children consumed in regard to media—movies, television, and music. We were fortunate that our children included Christian music in their libraries, and we encouraged their decision to listen to it. We were fairly strict in monitoring what television shows or movies we would allow, often earning for ourselves the title of "mean parents" compared to those of their friends. Our adult kids are divided in their opinions over whether we were too strict or got it about right.

But we realized we had to offer positive alternatives as well as set limits. We would spend time doing activities as a family, such as yardwork, cleaning, and cooking. Claire taught each of the children how to cook, and as the kids got older, they often had a night of the week on which they helped to make dinner. John taught them how to clean, having worked for years as a janitor in a Catholic hospital, and help with the lawn and garden.

But many of our shared activities were aimed at having fun. We tried to encourage art and forms of play that stimulated our kids' imaginations. Games were a favorite way to spend time together—board games, cards, and ping pong were favorites. Our only downfall was a competitive streak that we all shared and that could derail the fun if we let it get out of hand. We also read as a family—including reading together. When the kids were young, long car trips for family vacations were an opportunity to read longer books out loud—works by Tolkien, C. S. Lewis, and Richard Adams. This helped fuel the fires of our kids' imaginations and ensure that they all became avid readers on their own. When our kids were younger, we read to them before or after evening prayer as a family, before they went to bed. As they got older, the challenge was prying books out of their hands so that they could go to sleep.

### Family and Community

Though it is true that the Christian family is a domestic church, families need the support of the larger Christian community to fulfill their mission. A few generations ago, it was possible to count on a certain amount of support from the wider culture in reinforcing the basic values of Judeo-Christian morality. This is no longer true. On the far side of the sexual revolution, many people see no necessary connection between sex, marriage, and children. The contraceptive technology that powered the revolution offered the promise of sex without consequences—i.e., one could have sex with no fear of pregnancy or the need for marriage.

On the flip side, artificial reproductive technologies enable couples or even individuals to have children without either marriage or sexual union. Widespread divorce, itself a bitter fruit of the sexual revolution, has caused many people to fear and avoid marriage altogether. Many commentators argue that we now live in a post-marriage culture.[9]

The extended family has also been a traditional support for Christian families, but this support system has eroded in the United States and in much of the rest of the developed world. A few generations ago, young families in rural communities or ethnic city neighborhoods usually had a built-in support network of extended family living around them—grandparents, aunts, uncles, siblings—all of whom would have offered mentoring, support, and assistance in the daily tasks of raising children or caring for elderly relatives. This support would have been especially crucial in times of crisis such as illness, unemployment, or the death of a family member. For many families without this support system—for example, young immigrant families without extended family—close-knit ethnic communities who lived and worshipped together in the parish would step in to offer similar kinds of resources. Families not only prayed together in church but lived, worked, and played side by side with others who were striving to live out the same faith.

Large parishes in urban and suburban communities in the United States or other areas of the industrialized world often

---

9 For a brilliant overview of the damage wrought by the sexual revolution on the culture of the West, see Mary Eberstadt, *Adam and Eve after the Pill: Paradoxes of the Sexual Revolution* (San Francisco: Ignatius, 2012).

struggle to offer this kind of experience of community life to their members. People are more mobile and less likely to stay near their families of origin or their home parish. As a result, parishes and neighborhoods are in flux and sometimes unable to offer the common identity found when a population is more stable. Families with their own busy lives may look on their parish as a kind of sacramental service station where they drive in for a fill up of grace on Sundays and drive out again without knowing or interacting with those in the pews around them. In response to this development, some Catholics have sought and found Christian community outside of their parishes in lay ecclesial movements such as Opus Dei, the charismatic renewal, Focalare, the Neocatechumenal way, Communion and Liberation, and others. Such movements have been a grace for many in the Church in recent decades, enabling them to build a network of supportive Christian friendships and share their lives more deeply with others.

Given our individualistic culture, community does not just happen—it must be sought and lived intentionally. This has implications for our parishes. Pope Francis teaches that the parish is called to be "a community of communities, a sanctuary where the thirsty come to drink in the midst of their journey, and a center of constant missionary outreach."[10] The Holy Father's words point to some key ways to revitalize parish life in order to make them more authentic Christian communities. First, small faith-sharing groups play a key role in making a parish a "community

10 *Evangelii Guadium*, no. 28.

of communities." These can take the form of RCIA groups, Bible Studies, ministry teams, or support groups of various kinds. These groups enable people to build friendships and share their lives with others outside of their families. The Sunday liturgy can then be a coming together of a community of communities who are increasingly formed into the body of Christ by the Body of Christ which they receive.

Second, the parish must be a place of active hospitality where all are made welcome and accepted in love—regardless of their educational background, wealth, racial or ethnic identity, or personal history. The parish can then, much like a family, provide a "sanctuary" from the wider culture in the journey of conversion which is the Christian life. Third and finally, the parish must equip its members to be missionaries who invite others to encounter Christ the Great Physician and experience the healing that he offers—hence, parishes must be centers of evangelization.

But someone might ask, "Aren't our families themselves Christian communities?" If they are, why do they need other small communities in the larger Church? As a cell or one part of the body needs to be connected to all of the other parts of the body in order to flourish, the same holds for a Christian family. Men, women, and children of any age need friendships outside of the walls of their home in order to meet the full range of their interpersonal needs. Just as the myth of a soul mate who meets all of one's emotional and other needs can be lethal to a marriage, the idea of the self-enclosed Christian family that needs no support from others is illusory and even dangerous. To be a Christian means that one is committed to learning to live as a member of Christ's body, recognizing his or her dependence on the rest of that body. This is true for families as well as individuals. We need the witness, encouragement, and challenge provided by other people and other families to grow in holiness as we journey toward heaven.

### Our Search for Community

Even before we were married, we received a lesson as undergraduates in the importance of Christian community. The University of Steubenville strongly encouraged students to join men's and women's households. These were similar in some ways to Christ-centered fraternities and sororities—they functioned, too, as small faith-sharing groups. We not only joined households (Claire actually helped start one) but we served as coordinators of our households and eventually in campus-wide leadership of these groups.

The experience was formative for us. We learned the importance of Christian friendships with members of our own sex and enjoyed a kind of Christian brotherhood and sisterhood that we had not yet experienced given that we are the youngest in our families by many years and that Claire had no sisters. Sharing a range of activities such as intramural sports, on and off campus service activities, prayer, and social activities helped form strong friendships, some of which have endured. It also showed us the value of sharing our lives with other Christians on a deeper level.

We have continued to be intentional in seeking out Christian community. We've become involved in parishes where others wanted to share their lives beyond the opportunities afforded by liturgical participation and catechetical formation of our children. We've also become involved in groups within and outside of parish life where we found opportunities to grow in community. While in graduate school, for example, we joined a small Ignatian-based charismatic prayer community in Milwaukee. The friendships we formed there were an immense help during those stressful years of graduate school and early parenthood. Many of these men and women had been married much longer and had more experience raising children, and so their insights were an enormous blessing for us during these foundational years for our family.

In turn, as the youngest couple in the group by a number of years, we were able to inject an element of fun by adding social events like talent shows and seder meals into the community's life. We received and gave as members of the group and were blessed in the process. Neither this group nor other lay groups that we have been part of over the years have been perfect—far from it. The Church, like our families, is made up of imperfect people who fail and fall short. This is why patience and mutual forgiveness is a constant and necessary part of our life together in the body of Christ (cf. Col 3:12–13).

In addition to seeking out community in and outside of parishes to which we have belonged, we have also tried to help build it. The post-Cana group we started, at the invitation of our pastor, is an example of community building, in this case to help married couples support each other in living out their marriages. We started this ministry as an event-based opportunity, meeting monthly to foster faith formation, fellowship, and fun among couples. (We found that including another "f"—namely, food—helped our efforts and increased participation.) We offered theology on tap-type lectures, had movie and discussion nights, and sponsored romantic dinners for couples around Valentine's Day.

After trying this approach for a number of years and not seeing the results we had hoped for, we decided to try something different. Having fun together was good, but what couples needed was deeper exposure to Scripture and the Church's vision of marriage, along with an opportunity to pray and discuss in small groups the challenges and blessings of marriage and family life. We switched our approach and offered formation classes that included a talk, followed by a sharing from a couple, and then small group discussion. This format, though not original,[11] seems to be bearing more fruit, both in slowly increasing our ministry team and in building a greater number of supportive relationships among couples and families in the parish. We are glad to be able to share with others what we have learned through experience: we need the support of other Christians to thrive as a couple and as a family.

## Key Points

- Based on New Testament usage and early Christian teaching, the Church sees the family as a miniature church.

[11] The format is very similar to that of the Christ Life series used in many Catholic parishes. For more information, see "ChristLife Series," ChristLife Catholic Ministry for Evangelization, accessed February 20, 2017, https://christlife.org/christlife-series.

- The Christian family is a sanctuary—both in the sense of being a refuge from destructive influences and a holy place.
- There is less cultural support for marriage and families in Western culture than there was a few generations ago.
- Families need the support of the wider Christian community and other families in order to flourish.

8

# Praying as a Family

As we saw in the previous chapter, Christians see the family as a domestic church. One way to think of this is to see the family as a church in miniature whereby all of the activities of the body of Christ as a whole find a corollary or representation in a Christian household. St. John Paul II, in his apostolic exhortation *Familiaris Consortio,* developed this understanding by speaking of the family's participation in the threefold offices (*munera*) of Christ as priest, prophet, and king. In this chapter, we will focus on the priestly character of the family or what Pope St. John Paul II described as being "a community in dialogue with God."[1] Upcoming chapters will look at the family's participation in the other offices of the Lord Jesus.

The priesthood of the Christian family is first exercised at the couple's wedding. The Western or Latin understanding of the sacrament is that the couple themselves serve as the ministers conferring the sacrament on each other. The deacon, priest, or bishop is simply an official witness on the Church's behalf. Thus Pope Francis remarks:

---

1 *Familiaris Consortio*, no. 50. He develops this in nos. 55–62.

> In the Church's Latin tradition, the ministers of the sacrament of marriage are the man and the woman who marry; by manifesting their consent and expressing it physically, they receive a great gift. Their consent and their bodily union are the divinely appointed means whereby they become "one flesh." By their baptismal consecration, they were enabled to join in marriage as the Lord's ministers and thus to respond to God's call.[2]

It is Baptism that conforms the couple to Christ the priest and enables them to act as the ministers of the sacrament. This priesthood, which is different from the ministerial priesthood exercised by the clergy, continues in the couple's life of prayer together and with their children.

The sacrament which a couple confers and receives in their wedding is not simply a one-time infusion of grace. The bond which unites them is an ongoing source of grace empowering them to love and care for each other, to forgive each other, and to face hardship together in the power of the Holy Spirit. It is thus an encounter with Jesus who then walks with them in their life together. Pope Francis explains, "The sacrament is not a 'thing' or a 'power,' for in it Christ himself 'now encounters Christian spouses. . . . He dwells with them, gives them the strength to take up their crosses and so follow him, to rise again after they have fallen, to

2 Pope Francis, *Amoris Laetitia*, no. 75. The Eastern Orthodox churches have a different understanding of the minister of the sacrament. In their view, the priest or bishop marries the couple by conferring the nuptial blessing of the Church on them.

forgive one another, to bear one another's burdens.' Christian marriage is a sign of how much Christ loved his Church in the covenant sealed on the cross, yet it also makes that love present in the communion of the spouses."[3]

It also capacitates them to welcome and form the children with whom God blesses them. Christian husbands and wives draw on the grace available to them in the sacrament of marriage in a new way when they enter into the responsibilities of parenthood.

This sacramental bond uniting the couple is continually strengthened by the family's participation in the sacramental life of the Church. In the sacrament of Reconciliation, family members are renewed in their baptismal call to holiness and receive the healing power of grace to overcome sin and the wounds inflicted by their own sins as well as those of others. In the Eucharist, the family encounters the "source and summit" of their life as Christians and are formed into the body of Christ which they are.[4] In receiving the Bread of Life (cf. Jn 6) and the Cup of Salvation, families are nourished with what the Fathers of the Church called "the medicine of immortality."[5]

---

3 *Amoris Laetitia*, no. 73 (citing CCC 1642).

4 The phrase is from the Second Vatican Council's Dogmatic Constitution on the Church *Lumen Gentium*, no. 11.

5 Saint Ignatius of Antioch, for example, in his letter to the Ephesians described the Eucharist as "the medicine of immortality, and the antidote which wards off death, but yields continuous life in union with Jesus Christ." *Letter to the Ephesians*, 20; the translation is from *Early Christian Fathers*, ed. Cyril Richardson (New York: Macmillan, 1970), p. 93.

## The Family as a Sanctuary of Prayer

In addition to discussing the family as domestic church, the last chapter also touched on the idea proposed by the Church that the family is a sanctuary—a holy place. When we think of a church or a part of a church as a sanctuary, we think of it as a place of prayer. Certainly, this ought to be true in our families as well.

The opening chapters of the first book of Samuel tell a moving story about a holy woman named Hannah. Hannah desperately wanted a child but was unable to conceive. She promised the Lord that if he gave her a child, she would devote him to the Lord's service, and she indeed did conceive a son. As she had promised, Hannah brought her infant son to the temple after he was weaned so that he could grow up in the Lord's service. St. John Chrysostom praises Hannah as a model for the Christian parents of his day because she put her child's spiritual well-being ahead of her own desire to have a child to raise and call her own.[6]

In chapter three, we read of the boy Samuel asleep in the temple at Shiloh, where the Ark of the Covenant was kept. God called to Samuel while he was sleeping. The boy ran to the elderly priest Eli and declared, "Here I am. You called me" (1 Sm 3:5). However, the priest responded: "I did not call you. . . . Go back to sleep (1 Sm 3:6). This happened two more times before the priest realized that the Lord was calling the boy. He then instructed him: "Go to sleep, and if you are called, reply, 'Speak, LORD, for your servant is

---

6 See "Homily 21 on Ephesians 6:1–4" in *On Marriage and Family Life*, pp. 65–72, esp. 68–69.

listening'" (1 Sm 3:9). Samuel returned to sleep but when the Lord called him again, he was ready: "the LORD came and stood there, calling out as before: Samuel, Samuel! Samuel answered, 'Speak, for your servant is listening'" (1 Sm 3:10).

From this biblical story, we can learn some important truths. First, God wants to speak to his people—to us and to our children. Second, it is important to consecrate our homes as sacred spaces. Whenever we have moved into a new apartment or home over the years, we have had priest friends come and bless the home with holy water and blessed salt. Our adult children have continued the practice with their apartments or houses. Sacred items and art—crucifixes, pictures of saints, icons, and other religious art—also help to consecrate a home, serving as reminders to cultivate a spirit of prayer.

Third, to view our families and the dwellings in which we live as sanctuaries means that there has to be time for things other than work and busyness, and there has to be quiet in order to pray. It is not accidental that Samuel heard the Lord calling him in the silence of the night. For adults and children to be able to pray in our busy, noisy world filled with media and technological distraction, we have to actively cultivate silence.[7] Fourth, though God desires to reveal himself to us and to our children, we have to be trained to listen for and recognize his voice as well as learn how to respond to that voice.

---

7 On this see the insightful work of Robert Cardinal Sarah, *The Power of Silence: Against the Dictatorship of Noise,* trans. Michael Miller (San Francisco: Ignatius, 2016).

## The Forgotten Half of Prayer

The *Catechism of the Catholic Church* offers a simple definition of prayer as "a raising of the mind and heart to God."[8] But there is an even more simple way to understand prayer—it is a conversation. That is, in prayer we speak to God and he speaks to us. Many Christians focus on the first half of this conversation so intently that they lose sight of the second. Or some, under the influence of our secular culture, believe that God does not speak to us or that if he did during biblical times, he no longer does today. This is a false view of God which can be deadly to our spiritual lives.

When we pray, we can, and do, speak to God in a variety of modes: in quiet adoration, in worship, in thanksgiving (for example, for answered prayer), in repentance for our sins, and in intercession for others or petition for our needs. But God also speaks to *us* if we have the spiritual ears to hear. God speaks to us in the liturgy. He speaks to us when we prayerfully read Scripture. He can use our imaginations to speak to us in meditative prayer. He can move us through experiences of consolation and desolation. God can speak to us in contemplative prayer, in a silence deeper than words. And he can also speak to us through other people—through family, friends, mentors, spiritual directors, and even strangers.

As parents, it is crucial that we communicate to our children the importance of prayer and of cultivating both sides of the conversation. We can do this by teaching them to pray when they are young. Instilling in them a habit of daily

8 Cf. CCC 2259.

prayer and modeling for them the importance of periods of silence when praying (as their age and attentions spans allow) teaches them to be ready, like Samuel, to respond when the Lord speaks to them. These periods of silence can be part of a family examination of conscience or a prayerful response to Scripture reading. The value of silence is reinforced when we help children show reverence as they participate in liturgical worship and the prayer of the Church and teach them to cultivate the expectation that God will speak to them there. As children get older, parents should encourage them to develop their own prayer lives and show them how to do this. Such prayer ought to include talking to God in worship, repentance, and intercession, and listening to him in prayerful reading of Scripture and in periods of silence.

Parents can encourage teens to make time for more extended prayer—Eucharistic adoration and retreats are excellent opportunities for teens to encounter the Lord and deepen their relationship with him. Teens should also receive a deeper catechesis on the prayer of the Church in the form of a fuller understanding of the sacraments—not simply the sacrament of Confirmation for which they may be preparing—and the liturgy.

### Bringing the Liturgy Home

A friend who has done prison ministry once remarked that Catholics in prison have an advantage over imprisoned Christians from churches that do not structure their lives around the liturgy. For Christians from these non-liturgically focused churches, every day is like every other day and there is nothing to break the monotony of incarceration. However, for Catholics, Orthodox Christians, and other liturgically-focused Christian communities, every day is different. There are feast days and fast days, saints' days, and holy days. The Church gives us whole seasons such as Advent or Lent that are devoted to preparation for her great feasts.[9] When one enters into the rhythm of the liturgical seasons, the days are demarcated from each other with brightly colored hues. Personal prayer—even in a jail cell—takes on these hues and marks times and seasons as fundamentally different rather than as an endless parade of monotonous days.

This appreciation for the variety of the Church's seasons and feasts should be just as evident in the sanctuary that is the Christian family. Families who enter into the seasons of the liturgy enrich their own prayer together as they look for ways to "do more" in their prayer during seasons of penance and preparation such as Advent and Lent. They can read a Scripture text or do a brief evening prayer as a family before dinner. They can pray family Rosaries or other devotions. Or they might spend time as a family serving outside of their home in their parish or community. A family could choose to eat more simply during Lent and use the money saved to increase their sacrificial giving to the poor. Such

---

9 The medieval Western Church observed a second "little Lent" in addition to Advent. This was Whitsun week—a week of fasting which followed Pentecost and the Easter season and helped the faithful acclimate again to ordinary time. In the liturgy of some Syriac Orthodox churches, there were as many as seventeen periods of fasting in the liturgical year.

fasting need not only be from food—it can also be from media, whether social media or entertainment. Parents can use Advent wreaths or the Jesse tree to help children visualize the season and understand more deeply the meaning of the Incarnation in light of Christ's fulfillment of Old Testament promises and prophecies.

The great feasts that follow these periods of preparation can then be appreciated in a deeper way than their often trivial commemoration in the wider culture. Christmas is not just a time to put up decorations—often weeks or months before the day—and give and receive gifts, a practice co-opted and exploited by the commercialism of our consumer culture. It is the great feast of the Lord's nativity when God became man so that we could become sharers in the divine nature (cf. 2 Pt 1:4).

Easter is not about bunnies, hidden eggs, and jelly beans, but is the greatest of all feasts—the celebration of the Lord's resurrection from the dead which defeated the powers of sin, death, and the devil. This feast is so important that it cannot be contained by a single day but overflows into an eight-day celebration that culminates in Divine Mercy Sunday. Bringing the power and beauty of the liturgy and its seasons and symbols into the home can have a profound effect on the imaginations of children. This creates fertile soil for their prayer lives and their deepening lives of faith.

## Praying With Our Children

We were blessed to have encountered the Lord in a personal way before we entered marriage. In college, priests and professors encouraged us to make time for prayer on a daily basis—usually starting and ending the day with prayer. We learned a simple structure to use during this personal prayer time. First, we began with praise and gratitude for God's goodness. This could include singing hymns, reading psalms, or just expressing praise and gratitude to God for his goodness. Second, we did an examination of conscience and repented of our sins. Third, we read Scripture and spent time listening for the voice of God, genuinely expecting that he would speak to us. Fourth, we spent time interceding for ourselves and others. The structure is not unique and it is well-supported in Scripture and in the liturgical tradition of the Church.[10]

Even before our marriage, we actively shared our prayer lives with each other. We did this by spending time talking about what we were learning in our prayer and what God was teaching us. We would also pray together occasionally. After our marriage, we started praying together more regularly. At first, this meant we would pray together one day a week instead of having individual prayer times. Over time, we found ourselves praying together more as we woke together and began our day in prayer. Before our children were born or when they were very young, this usually meant the very first thing in morning when the house was quiet.

---

10 Thus the Our Father contains the elements of praise ("hallowed be thy name"), repentance ("forgive us our trespasses"), seeking guidance ("lead us not into temptation" and "thy will be done"), and intercession ("deliver us from evil" and "give us this day our daily bread"). See Mt 6:9–13. Night prayer in the Church's Liturgy of the Hours contains the same basic elements and structure.

We would use the time to sit together, drink coffee, and begin our day with prayer.

As our children grew older and more of them came, things began to change. Little faces would appear in our bedroom and gather at the foot of our bed. We realized that we had a choice to make. We could try to shoo them away so we could have a few more minutes of quiet, we could stop praying when they showed up and simply plunge into our hectic days, or we could include them in our prayer. We began to see that this was a wonderful opportunity to teach our children about prayer by doing it with them. So John would get out his guitar, and we would sing songs with the children. We read Bible stories or lives of the saints together and encouraged them to reflect on what God was saying to us. And we took time to pray for people and for things that were happening that day.

Our children also saw us taking time in our own personal prayer to listen to God and write in prayer journals what we felt he was saying to us. As they grew older, we encouraged them to do the same in their own prayer.

Like many families, we prayed with our children before they went to bed at night. Over time, we found that this was a good moment to do a family examination of conscience—asking forgiveness of God and one another for ways that we had hurt each other that day. It was important for our children to see their father and mother acknowledge their sins and to ask their forgiveness when we fell short as parents and as Christians. Our children could see that daily reconciliation is part of life together as Christians. St. Paul's letter to the Ephesians tells us that this is something we should do before sleep: "Be angry but do not sin; do not let the sun set on your anger, and do not leave room for the devil" (Eph 4:26–27). As our children grew older, we began to pray night prayer from the Liturgy of the Hours with them and discovered that the Church includes this text every Wednesday evening. Commenting on this text, Pope Francis teaches:

> My advice is never to let the day end without making peace in the family. "And how am I going to make peace? By getting down on my knees? No! Just by a small gesture, a little something, and harmony within your family will be restored. Just a little caress, no words are necessary.
>
> But do not let the day end without making peace in your family". Our first reaction when we are annoyed should be one of heartfelt blessing, asking God to bless, free and heal that person. "On the contrary bless, for to this you have been called, that you may obtain a blessing" (1 Pet 3:9).

Pope Francis's words contain a great deal of wisdom. Reconciliation in our families should be a daily occurrence. And praying for those who offend or annoy us is a great defense against allowing the poison of resentment to take root in our hearts.

### Discernment

Scripture and the Church's tradition tell us that we can expect God to speak to us when we create the space and time for him to do so in our homes and hearts. However, as the story of Samuel asleep in the temple makes clear, we do not always recognize his voice when it comes to us. We might also confuse other voices we hear within us for the voice of God.

Another famous biblical story makes the point in dramatic fashion. In 1 Kings 19, the great prophet Elijah flees from the wrath of Queen Jezebel into the desert and with angelic assistance makes his way to Mount Horeb (called Mount Sinai in other biblical stories). Waiting there in a cave, he experiences great signs such as heralded God's revelation of himself to Moses and the Israelites on the same mountain in Exodus—"a strong and violent wind," "an earthquake," and "fire" (see 1 Kgs 19:11–12; cf. Ex 19:16–19; 33:18–23). But God is not in any of those manifestations. It is only in a "light silent sound" that God communicates the reality of his presence to the prophet. The Hebrew phrase *ḏaqqāh dəmāmāh qōw*, sometimes translated "still small voice," is paradoxical. What is a "silent sound" or a "still voice"? The paradox points to an experience common in the life of prayer. God speaks and reveals himself to us in ways that are sometimes unexpected or mysterious. We do not control God or the way he chooses to speak to us. But what we can do is make ourselves available and train our spiritual perception to recognize his voice when he does speak.

The art of training our spiritual ears to listen for the voice of the Lord and to distinguish his voice from other voices and impulses is known as discernment. St. Ignatius Loyola, the founder of the Society of Jesus (the Jesuits), is the great teacher of discernment in the Christian tradition. Saint Ignatius recognized that many of the voices we hear within do not come from God—some can be rooted in our fears or self-interest, some might come from worldly influences around us, and some might be temptations from evil spirits. Nonetheless, Ignatius believed that God does speak to us, and he developed several methods and an intensive retreat program to help people grow in their ability to hear God's voice and recognize the movements of the Holy Spirit within their souls.[11]

In some cases, the source of an inclination that we receive in prayer is not immediately clear. We might need to begin to act on it in order to judge the source by the fruit that it bears in our lives. When we are seeking God's guidance for particularly important questions, we should gather wisdom and input from others experienced in the spiritual life—priests, spiritual directors, mentors, or other mature Christians with strong prayer lives.

We have found as a couple that we tend to discern very differently. This first became clear to us while we were engaged and discerning where John should go to graduate school and hence where we would live during our first years of marriage. At the time, this seemed disconcerting—even alarming. However, over time, we realized that though we discern differently, when we both really listen, the Lord guides us to a common understanding.

Claire will spend time in prayer and then simply state that God put something in her heart or made something clear. When pressed, she cannot always articulate reasons for her

---

11 See Ignatius of Loyola, *The Spiritual Exercises*, ed. Luis Puhl, S.J. (Chicago: The Newman Press, 1951).

judgment, but she can often point to a certitude and peace about God's will in a given situation. John is much more at home in some of the methods of Ignatian discernment. A particular favorite is Ignatius's method of stating a question both positively and negatively and listing all of the pros and cons. Praying over these lists often allows the Holy Spirit the opportunity to surface some of the fears and selfishness that underlie individual thoughts about outcomes. For a "head" person, this can serve to quiet the mind and shed light on the spirits or voices that are not from God. This can create space to hear the "still small voice of God" amid the other voices which we hear. We have also found that it is important to pray daily for God's guidance and that we know his will; this practice helps us hear him speak through other persons, events, or situations.

As our children have gotten older, they have occasionally asked us about how we seek God's will in specific situations or shared with us some of their own processes of discernment. We have encouraged them to cultivate that habit of listening for the Lord in their prayer lives and, in some cases, we have served as sounding boards as they discerned things like graduate school, the choice of a state in life, and the choice of a spouse. We also encouraged them to seek guidance from others in navigating these decisions. Discernment is an art—not a science. In our fallen world in which we walk by faith, we "see indistinctly, as in a mirror" lacking the "face to face" vision of heaven, as Saint Paul tells us (see 1 Cor 13:12). Sometimes we listen to the wrong voice or make wrong turns. The good news is that God's mercy is always available to us when we fail. He is always ready to speak to us anew, and even when we make wrong turns in pursuing God's plan for our lives, he is able to get us back on course. For ourselves and for our children, God's mercies are new every morning (cf. Lam 3:22–23).

## Key Points

- We are called to make our homes sanctuaries of prayer.
- God speaks to us when we pray, but we need to cultivate our ability to listen and to teach our children to do the same.
- Entering into the liturgy in our family life is a great way to cultivate prayer in our homes and families.
- The art of listening for God's voice and distinguishing it from other voices in and outside of us is called discernment.

9

# Serving as a Family

On the mantle in our family room sits a print replica of Ford Madox Brown's painting of Jesus washing Peter's feet. In the foreground, Jesus kneels before Peter, washing his feet in a basin of water and drying them with a towel wrapped around him. Peter glowers at Jesus, apparently still stung by the rebuke he had received. When Jesus approached Peter to wash his feet, Peter had protested, "You will never wash my feet." To this Jesus responded, "Unless I wash you, you will have no inheritance with me" (Jn 13:8). In the background of the very compressed view, the other apostles peer in wonder or puzzlement at the dramatic scene unfolding before them. Like their leader Peter, they did not understand the prophetic nature of Jesus's action (cf. Jn 13:7)—how it foreshadowed his ultimate act of service in giving his life for us on the cross. Having completed his prophetic action of washing his followers' feet, Jesus said to the Twelve: "Do you realize what I have done for you? You call me 'teacher' and 'master,' and rightly so, for indeed I am. If I, therefore, the master and teacher, have washed your feet, you ought to wash one another's feet. I have given you a model to follow, so that as I have done for you, you should also do" (Jn

13:12–15). Jesus thus links service to discipleship. If we are his followers, we are called to serve others.

The Ford Madox Brown print is particularly meaningful to us because the Gospel reading we chose for our wedding Mass was the washing of the feet (Jn 13:1–17). We selected it because John used it when he proposed to Claire. In a gesture equal parts pious, romantic, and naïve, he read the Gospel text, knelt, and washed Claire's feet, and then asked if he could do this for the rest of our lives. Before kneeling and washing her feet, he even repeated Jesus's statement, "What I am doing, you do not understand now, but you will understand later" (Jn 13:7). Neither of us realized at the time that this Gospel passage was indeed prophetic of our marriage and future family life. Like Peter and the apostles, we had (and have) much to learn about service, the gift of suffering, and the transformation of authority into sacrificial service by Jesus.

## Authority in a Fallen World

One of the effects of sin is the breakdown of harmonious relationships into antagonism and the struggle for power and control. This is evident in Scripture from the creation accounts of Genesis onward. One of the first places that this becomes evident is in the relationship between the sexes. Men and women were created fundamentally equal in nature and dignity and called to covenantal unity in marriage. But they deformed their relationship by their act of rebellion against God. God's words to the woman after the sin of our first parents graphically describe the disorder: "Your urge shall be for your husband, and he shall rule over you" (Gn 3:16). St. John Paul II read these words as descriptive of male domination of and exploitation of women in the family and in society down through history. He writes:

> We discover a break and a constant threat precisely in regard to this "unity of the two" which corresponds to the dignity of the image and likeness of God in both of them. But this threat is more serious for the woman, since domination takes the place of "being a sincere gift" and therefore living "for" the other: "he shall rule over you". This "domination" indicates the disturbance and loss of the stability of that fundamental equality which the man and the woman possess in the "unity of the two": and this is especially to the disadvantage of the woman. . . .
>
> These words of Genesis refer directly to marriage, but indirectly they concern the different spheres of social life: the situations in which the woman remains disadvantaged or discriminated against by the fact of being a woman.[1]

That is, in our fallen world, some men have used their greater physical strength and women's vulnerability during pregnancy and the care of young children to exploit them for their own selfish ends—both in marriage and in society. For St. John Paul II, this male "rule" over women is not God's plan for marriage and the family but the result of human sin.

---

1 *Mulieris Dignitatem*, no. 10.

A similar disordering of relationships can be seen in the political sphere. God intended that the people of Israel, his covenant people, would be different from the nations around them. One aspect of his plan was that he alone would be their king. He would govern them through the *torah*, the instruction he had given in the covenants he had made with them. The people, however, wanting to emulate the nations around them, called for a human king. God told the prophet Samuel: "Listen to whatever the people say. You are not the one they are rejecting. They are rejecting me as their king" (1 Sm 8:7). At God's direction, Samuel warned them that a king would tax, oppress, and ultimately enslave them with his despotic rule (see 1 Sm 8:10–18). The people, however, replied, "'No! There must be a king over us. We too must be like all the nations, with a king to rule us, lead us in warfare, and fight our battles" (1 Sm 8:19–20).

This defection from God's rule reaches a crescendo in the Gospel of John when the religious leaders of the Jewish people, in order to manipulate Pilate into condemning Jesus, declare, "We have no king but Caesar" (Jn 19:15). In complying with their demand, Pilate unwittingly declares the true identity of Jesus, the true king of Israel who reigns from the cross, posting an inscription that stated: "Jesus the Nazorean, the King of the Jews" (Jn 19:19). In his sacrificial offering of himself, Jesus reveals the true nature of authority and transforms the way it is to be exercised among his followers.

### Authority Exercised Through Service

When Jesus sees his own apostles jockeying for positions of power and influence, he challenges them with a radically different view of authority from that of the world. "Jesus summoned them and said to them, 'You know that those who are recognized as rulers over the Gentiles lord it over them, and their great ones make their authority over them felt. But it shall not be so among you. Rather, whoever wishes to be great among you will be your servant; whoever wishes to be first among you will be the slave of all. For the Son of Man did not come to be served but to serve and to give his life as a ransom for many'" (Mk 10:42–45). Among the followers of Jesus, the quest for power and control over others has no place. Authority has to be exercised as sacrificial service, as Jesus did in offering himself for us.

The Church is not primarily a political organization in the sense of a nation state.[2] In her own interior life as "the People of God" and "the body of Christ," she strives to organize herself according to the teaching of her Lord for whom "to serve is to reign."[3] It is for this reason that the popes since Gregory the Great have used the title "Servant of the Servants of God" (*Servus servorum Dei*) to describe themselves. The ministries of the other members of the hierarchy (such

2 Though this has not always been recognized uniformly in the past as some of the history of the Papal States makes clear.

3 This is an ancient Christian axiom which can be found in official documents of the Church. See, for example, the Second Vatican Council's Dogmatic Constitution on the Church in the Modern World, *Lumen Gentium*, no. 36.

as bishops) are likewise ordered to the service of the Church as a whole. As Pope Francis explains:

> But in this Church, as in an inverted pyramid, the top is located beneath the base. Consequently, those who exercise authority are called "ministers", because, in the original meaning of the word, they are the least of all. It is in serving the people of God that each bishop becomes, for that portion of the flock entrusted to him, *vicarius Christi*, the vicar of that Jesus who at the Last Supper bent down to wash the feet of the Apostles (cf. Jn 13:1-15).[4]

This transformation of authority into service should not only characterize the life of the Church, it should also be reflected in the domestic Church that is the family. Thus the letter to the Ephesians, in elaborating the "headship" of the husband, describes it in this way: "Husbands, love your wives, even as Christ loved the church and handed himself over for her to sanctify her, cleansing her by the bath of water with the word" (Eph 5:25–26). Again, the sacrificial love of Christ manifested on the cross becomes the norm and even the source of the love within marriage.[5] This fact, along with the explicit call to "be subordinate to one another out of reverence for Christ" which opens and frames the passage, led

---

4 Pope Francis, "Address at the Ceremony Commemorating the 50th Anniversary of the Institution of the Synod of Bishops" (October 17, 2015).

5 Note that the word for love here is *agape*—a word used throughout the New Testament to describe a reality originating in God (cf. 1 Jn 4:10) and fully disclosed and communicated in the cross of Christ (cf. Rom 5:8).

St. John Paul II to teach that the passage demonstrates the mutual authority of husband and wife exercised in sacrificial service to one another.[6] If husband and wife freely subordinate themselves to Christ, one cannot be in servile subjection to the other. The wounds in the relationship of men and women opened by sin as described in Genesis 3 can thus be healed by the grace at work within Christian marriage.

For St. John Paul II, there is also an element of mutuality interjected into the relationship between Christian parents and children. The commandment directed to children to "honor your father and mother" (Ex 20:12; Dt 5:16; Eph 6:2) also implies a certain kind of reciprocity. Children are first and foremost God's children, made in his image and likeness, and parents must recognize this reality. At the very least, says St. John Paul II, parents are called to acknowledge their children, to listen to them, and to respect their dignity in the process of educating them in love.[7] The obedience which children owe their parents "in the Lord" (cf. Eph 6:1) presupposes that parents use their authority for the good of their children—that is, to serve them.

### Family as a School of Service and Love

The Christian family's participation in the kingly office of Christ is expressed in service in and outside of their home. As St. John Paul II puts it, the family is called to be "a community at the service of man."[8] This is lived out by putting

---

6 See *Mulieris Dignitatem*, no. 24.

7 See his reflections on the fourth commandment in his 1994 Letter to Families, *Gratissimam Sane*, nos. 15–16.

8 *Familiaris Consortio*, no. 50.

into daily practice Jesus's commandment of love. Speaking of husbands and wives, the Letter to the Ephesians says: "So [also] husbands should love their wives as their own bodies. He who loves his wife loves himself" (Eph 5:28). One hears in these words the second half of the Great Commandment of the Gospels: "Love your neighbor as yourself" (cf. Lv 19:18; Mk 12:31; Mt 22:39; Lk 10:27). In other words, one's first neighbor is one's spouse and children.

The fabric of a family's daily life is comprised of a host of simple gestures of love and service. As Pope Francis puts it:

> Like happiness, holiness is always tied to little gestures. "Whoever gives you a cup of water in my name will not go unrewarded," says Jesus (cf. Mk 9:41). These little gestures are those we learn at home, in the family; they get lost amid all the other things we do, yet they do make each day different.
>
> They are the quiet things done by mothers and grandmothers, by fathers and grandfathers, by children, by brothers and sisters. They are little signs of tenderness, affection and compassion. Like the warm supper we look forward to at night, the early lunch awaiting someone who gets up early to go to work. Homely gestures. Like a blessing before we go to bed, or a hug after we return from a hard day's work. Love is shown by little things, by attention to small daily signs which make us feel at home.[9]

---

9 Homily at the Closing Mass of the Eighth World Meeting of Families in Philadelphia (September 27, 2015).

To the things which the Holy Father mentions we could add many others: paying bills, taking care of a sick spouse or child, household chores, preparing meals, washing dishes or laundry, carpooling, juggling schedules—all of the things families do for one another in the course of their daily lives.

Yet this service cannot stop at the walls of a family's house—it must reach out into the wider community to assist others in need. As Saint John Paul II expressed it, "The spouses together as a couple, the parents and children as a family, must live their service to the Church and to the world. They must be 'of one heart and soul' in faith, through the shared apostolic zeal that animates them, and through their shared commitment to works of service to the ecclesial and civil communities."[10]

In other words, the neighbors we are called to love are not simply those with whom we live. In the parable of the sheep and the goats (Mt 25:31–46), Jesus identifies himself with the hungry, the thirsty, the stranger, the naked, and the imprisoned. Families are called to discover and minister to Jesus in what St. Teresa of Calcutta called his "distressing disguise of the poor."[11] Sometimes this poverty to which we are called to respond takes the form of loneliness, or the suffering of those in broken or hurting families. Families who reach out to meet these needs of others through the practice of the corporal works of mercy (cf. CCC 2447) usually find that they in fact receive far more than they give. As they

---

10 *Familiaris Consortio*, no. 50.

11 Mother Teresa, *In the Heart of the World: Thoughts, Stories and Prayers* (Novato, CA: New World Library, 2010), p. 23.

serve vulnerable or disadvantaged members of their communities, they encounter Christ in those they serve.

The family's mission of love expressed through service is reflected and sustained liturgically. The very ordinary gifts of bread and wine offered in the Eucharistic liturgy symbolize the daily work, sustenance, and joys of the families gathered around the altar. Christ then transforms this daily toil and joy into his own real presence in the Eucharistic elements. Families thus find themselves both offered and transformed by the Eucharist. If Baptism is the foundation of the Christian family's vocation to holiness, the Eucharist is its source and summit.

Pope Benedict XVI pointed out that the love of God of which we partake in the Eucharist—like all authentic love, human and divine—is both *agape* (Christ's sacrificial self-gift to us) and *eros* (reflecting and realizing God's passionate desire to be one with us). Our participation in the Eucharist in turn empowers us to put love into concrete action in and outside of our families.[12] Transformed by the Body of Christ which we share, we can then encounter him in those we serve.

This practice of loving service in and outside of our homes is one of the primary ways we form and prepare our children for their future vocations. Helping them to develop a prayer life is how we assist them in hearing the Lord's voice when he

---

12 See Benedict XVI, encyclical *Deus Caritas Est,* nos. 13–14. Note that in the New Testament era, *eros* did not have the connotations we associate with the "erotic." It meant a passionate desire for union. Sexual desire or lust was described by the Greek word *epithumia.*

calls them; learning to serve is what shapes their character so that they are able to form Christian friendships and to make a definitive commitment to care for and love others in marriage and parenthood. Service develops the cardinal virtues of temperance, fortitude, and justice and their related virtues such as chastity, patience, and mercy. For Christians, all of these virtues are unified and animated by charity, which is infused in us as a gift of grace by the Holy Spirit. We love because we have first been loved by the Father in the gift of his Son (cf. 1 Jn 4:10).

## Learning to Serve Together

When we married, we understood that it was important to serve one another, but thirty-three years of marriage and the challenges we have encountered along the way have certainly helped us realize this more deeply.

Our first years of marriage were a kind of trial by fire in this regard. Pregnant with our first child four months after our wedding, Claire was constantly sick during her first year of full-time teaching at a Catholic grade school. John, struggling through his first year of graduate school, found himself scrambling to take care of Claire, manage our household, and keep up with his doctoral classes. This meant a lot of late nights cooking, cleaning, and studying. For Claire, it meant a struggle to let herself be served and loved. The birth of children added new challenges like sleep deprivation as children woke us during the night with hunger, sickness, or during teething. Learning to be responsible for little ones who were utterly dependent on us was a challenge and a joy, and we matured as a result.

As we've mentioned, we taught our children the importance of serving their family by helping around the house. Even when they were small, we enlisted them in simple tasks like a nightly toy patrol (or clean up) before dinner so that we could have a neat and relatively peaceful house. As they grew, we had weekly family cleaning days where everyone had responsibilities—from dusting or vacuuming the house, to washing the bathroom or the kitchen floor, to brushing dogs and stacking firewood. Everyone helped with the yard as well, some weeding gardens and others mowing the lawn. We were a family, and we expected everyone to help—in our case, this meant our boys in the same ways as the girls, and vice versa. Thus everyone took turns cleaning the bathroom and everyone helped mow the lawn; the key was that everyone chipped in to serve the family.

We also encouraged our kids to serve others beyond our family. We tried to set an example by helping prepare couples for marriage and by running the post-Cana marriage ministry at our parish. Many of our kids also engaged in service to the Church, teaching religious education to young children, doing peer ministry, or serving on the parish council. As a family, we've tried to have a ministry of hospitality, inviting others into our home for holiday celebrations—students, priests, and the elderly. In this we were following the example of Claire's parents who were two of the most generous and hospitable people we have known and who constantly welcomed Jesus to their home in the form of priests, the elderly, and the homeless.

Looking back, we can see that our service as a family outside of our home has been more episodic than a constant feature of our lives. We occasionally volunteered at soup kitchens, or prayed at abortion clinics, or assisted elderly neighbors, but we did these as opportunities arose rather than on a consistent basis. Thankfully, our kids found their own ways to serve, encouraged in part by their public high school which incentivized community service for things like the National Honors Society and thus reinforced the call to serve when we were less than consistent in doing so as parents.

We are grateful as parents to see that, in spite of our own inconsistencies and shortcomings, our children have repeatedly stepped up and served us during difficult periods in our family's life. About ten years ago, we went through a rather dark time as a family. We had both assumed the responsibilities of caring for our parents as they aged. We thus found ourselves in the role of "sandwich parents," struggling to care for elderly parents and our own teens and younger children at the same time. Then we lost a number of family members in the span of about two years—Claire's father, John's sister, and then his mother.

A few years earlier, John had torn a disc in his lower back and was dealing with chronic physical pain as well as battling depression and trying to medicate this pain with alcohol. During this stressful time, Claire developed an autoimmune disease that severely limited her ability to do much around the house or even to drive a car. To our grateful amazement, our kids stepped up in numerous ways—they helped us both get to doctors' appointments and pitched in more around the house without being asked. They drove her where she needed to go, went Christmas shopping for her, and then wrapped the gifts for our family Christmas celebration. We saw that they weren't just self-absorbed teenagers who were impervious to our efforts to teach them—they were able to put love into action through myriad acts of concrete service to our family.

Even as adults, our kids continue to step in and serve us when the need arises. Recently, Claire's mother was in the end stages of dementia. We and our children who were in the area had the privilege of spending hours with her before she died, praying the Rosary and the Divine Mercy chaplet in her room. After her death, once again we saw our children step up to serve us. While we focused on planning the funeral Mass, our oldest daughter organized her siblings to cover everything else that needed to be done. Our kids called all of our relatives and all of Claire's friends to tell them of her mother's passing. Once all of them arrived home prior to the funeral, they completely cleaned our house—they washed sheets for out of town guests, dusted, vacuumed, cleaned bathrooms, cleaned floors, and brushed the dogs. They not only planned the reception at church but they also planned the food for all of the extended family staying with us from breakfast through dinner. All the things we had taught them as children they now gave as a gift of love to us in remembrance of their Grandma Louise.

### The School of Suffering, Service, and Christian Hope

In *Spe Salvi,* his beautiful 2007 encyclical on hope, Pope Benedict XVI mentions specific settings for practicing and growing in the virtue. Among these are prayer (nos. 32–34) and suffering (nos. 36–39). His words ring true in the light of our own experience.

We have seen the importance of praying for opportunities to serve because God answers such prayers. Toward the tail end of that difficult period in our family's life, Claire was praying one day. Because we had both been ill, we weren't doing much to help others, and our kids and friends had in many ways been taking care of us. Claire told the Lord that she was ready to be the one to help others again. Specifically, she asked God for two things: first, to be able to serve the Church as a couple and, second, to go to Rome for our twenty-fifth wedding anniversary. Three months later, God answered both prayers in dramatic fashion. Claire was driving to work when John—who was at home recovering from back surgery—called to tell her that he was receiving email congratulations from around the country because we had been appointed to something. He wasn't sure what it was but said that he would find out. After a bit of investigation, he discovered that Pope Benedict XVI had appointed us as a member couple to the Pontifical Council on the Family. He called Claire back with the news. Her response conveyed her shock: "What do you mean *we*? Why me? What does this mean?" John responded, "I'm not completely sure, but *we* are going to serve the Church as a couple and *we* are going to Rome." Claire was flabbergasted—the first plenary session of the Pontifical Council that we would attend was held the year of our twenty-fifth anniversary. As she said later, "Only God could have answered my prayer so perfectly."

As we look back on the times of suffering that we have experienced in our family—through struggles in caring for parents, losing parents and siblings, battling pain and sickness—we can also see how these were also times of great blessing. As one of our children said to us at the time, "Those trials are making me into the person God wants me to be." During the times of struggle, we came to realize more deeply our need for God and his grace. We learned in a much deeper way what it means to serve and to be served. And we can draw on some of these lessons when we minister to other couples and families. We can see that the lessons of service which we tried to teach our children have helped form them into young men and women who desire to serve the Church and who have been visible signs of God's love and mercy to us.

The print of Jesus washing Peter's feet is a daily reminder of what is at the heart of our marriage and our family life as followers of Jesus. Like Peter, we still have much to learn about the true nature of what it means to live and love as a disciple. But like him, we have the opportunity to encounter the transforming love of Jesus who exercises his kingship among us in humble service. He is the true source of our hope. As Pope Benedict XVI writes, "In what does this hope consist which, as hope, is 'redemption'? The essence of the answer is given in the phrase from the Letter to the Ephesians. . . . The Ephesians, before their encounter with Christ, were without hope because they were 'without God in the world'. To come to know God—the true God—means to receive hope.[13]

### Key Points

- Because of the effects of sin, we often confuse authority with power to dominate or control others.
- Through his life, death, and resurrection, Jesus transforms the exercise of authority into sacrificial service. For Christians, "to serve is to reign."
- Learning to serve one another and to serve together is a way that a Christian family participates in the kingly office of Christ.
- Serving those who are suffering and being served by others while suffering are ways to practice and grow in Christian hope.

13 *Spe Salvi*, no. 3.

10

# Giving Witness as a Family

In addition to being conformed to Christ in his offices as priest and king, Christian families share in his office as prophet. Our families are called to give credible and joyful witness in word and deed. As parents, part of our task is to raise children who are capable of doing this.

In recent decades, the Church has increasingly seen the family as a center of evangelization. Saint Paul VI, in his 1976 apostolic exhortation *Evangelii Nuntiandi,* says, "The family, like the Church, ought to be a place where the Gospel is transmitted and from which the Gospel radiates. In a family which is conscious of this mission, all the members evangelize and all the members are evangelized. The parents not only communicate the Gospel to their children, but from their children they can themselves receive the same Gospel as deeply lived by them. And such a family becomes an evangelizer of many other families, and of the neighborhood of which it forms a part."[1]

All the members of the family, hearing the Word of God proclaimed by the Church and in their own lives of prayer, are called to speak that word to one another and to authenticate that proclamation by the witness of their lives. The

1 Paul VI, apostolic exhortation *Evangelii Nuntiandi*, no. 71.

Holy Father's appreciation for the evangelizing power of children is noteworthy and recalls Jesus's praise of children as models for discipleship in the Gospels. And the Christian family's task of giving testimony in word and deed does not stop at the walls of their home; it is meant to impact other families and the communities in which they live.

St. John Paul II concurs with the teaching of his predecessor. He states in *Familiaris Consortio* that "the future of evangelization depends in great part on the Church of the home."[2] This begins with the work of parents in evangelizing and catechizing their children. This work, he says, should be "interwoven with love, simplicity, practicality, and daily witness."[3] In other words, evangelization must be woven into the patterns and habits of daily life. It isn't something families only do on Sundays or at special times of the year. The aim of this evangelization and catechesis is to form children able to respond to God's call to them. He writes, "The family must educate children for life in such a way that each one may fully perform his or her role according to the vocation received from God."[4] In this way, we can understand that part of this evangelizing work comes through the practice of service discussed in the previous chapter.

Like all apostolic work, this work of evangelization in the home often entails suffering as when adolescent or adult children reject the faith they received as children or when families struggle to make their lives cohere with the faith they profess. Finally, St. John Paul II notes that this work

---

2 *Familiaris Consortio*, no. 52.

3 Ibid., no. 53.

4 Ibid.

is "essentially an ecclesial service," taking place within the Church "as an evangelized and evangelizing community."[5]

For Pope Francis, the ecclesial nature of the family's participation in the work of evangelization means that families themselves must take the lead in the Church's ministry to families. In his apostolic exhortation *Amoris Laetitia,* he writes, "The Synod Fathers emphasized that Christian families, by the grace of the sacrament of matrimony, are the principal agents of the family apostolate, above all through 'their joy-filled witness as domestic churches.' . . . Enabling families to take up their role as active agents of the family apostolate calls for 'an effort at evangelization and catechesis inside the family.'"[6]

Like St. John Paul II, Pope Francis emphasizes the importance of the catechesis of families so that they can carry out their evangelizing mission. Families must receive adequate formation so that they can form their own members as well as minister to other families. This is an extension of Pope Francis's insistence that all in the Church—laity as well as religious and clergy—are called to evangelize. In his apostolic exhortation *Evangelii Gaudium,* Pope Francis writes, "In virtue of their baptism, all of the members of the People of God have become missionary disciples." In the same section, he continues, "The new evangelization calls for personal involvement on the part of each and every one of the baptized. Every Christian is challenged, here and now, to be actively engaged in evangelization."[7]

---

5 Ibid.

6 *Amoris Laetitia*, no. 200.

7 *Evangelii Gaudium*, no. 120.

## The New Evangelization

The Church of the first centuries was not particularly influential in Roman society. Comprised of relatively unknown, poor, and largely uneducated people (cf. 1 Cor 1:26–29), the early Christians were regarded with suspicion and even overt hostility by their Jewish and pagan Roman neighbors. This hostility erupted in occasional bouts of savage persecution of followers of Jesus by Roman authorities. Yet in the fourth century, the situation of the Church changed dramatically. Constantine gave Christianity legal protection through the Edict of Milan in 313, and by century's end, it had been enshrined as the empire's official religion. The empire that had tried to conquer the Church and its Gospel was instead conquered by it. How did it happen? How did a small band of Christians turn the world of their time upside down?

The apostles, bishops, and priests who succeeded them spearheaded the first great evangelization. These men, on fire with the Holy Spirit and transformed by the love of Christ, laid down their lives in the work of evangelization, building up churches around the Mediterranean world and beyond. Periodic efforts by Roman authorities to crush this growing religion through coercion or bloody persecution only served to fan the flames of faith and highlight the power of the martyrs' testimony to it. As Tertullian famously wrote at the end of the second century, "The blood of the martyrs is the seed of the Church."[8]

The newfound prominence of the Church in Roman society was not enough to stem the crumbling political and

---

[8] Tertullian, *Apology*, 50. The Greek word *martyr* means "witness."

military strength of the western Latin-speaking portion of the empire. The movement of Germanic and other "barbarian" peoples into the territory of the empire overwhelmed its flagging resources and led to its collapse in the fifth and sixth centuries. The Church in these territories now found itself in a new and difficult situation dealing with these peoples, many of whom were pagan and some of whom had been converted and catechized by heretical Arian missionaries from the Greek-speaking East.

A second great evangelizing effort of the Church in the West took place in this context. In this case, the effort was centered in monasteries and spearheaded by monks. Monasteries preserved some of the learning and culture of the past (both pagan and Christian), but they were also centers of evangelization, catechesis, and Christian education. Around these centers of Christian life, the peoples of Europe were evangelized and the Christian civilization of the Middle Ages took root and then flowered.

The current situation of the Church at the beginning of the twenty-first century is significantly different. In the Western world, we are not dealing with peoples and cultures who have never heard the Gospel but increasingly with people who believe that they have heard the Christian message and have rejected it. That is, we now live in a post-Christian culture in the West. The imprint of Christianity has faded in many parts of an increasingly secular Europe. In the United States, studies show that the fastest growing religious group or affiliation in the country is those who claim to have none at all.[9]

---

9 See the summary of the Pew Research Center's 2014 Religious

This is the context in which recent popes—beginning with St. Paul VI—have begun to speak of a "new evangelization." In this they are reminding us of an essential characteristic of the Church entrusted with the good news of salvation. The Church—and all of her members—are called to evangelize. Pope Francis is simply making programmatic for the Church the teaching of his predecessors. Thus Pope Benedict XVI wrote in his first encyclical, "Being a Christian is not the result of an ethical choice or a lofty idea, but the encounter with an event, a person, which gives life a new horizon and a decisive direction."[10]

In his encyclical on moral theology, St. John Paul II made a striking claim in commenting on the encounter between the rich young man of Matthew 19: "*In order to make this 'encounter' with Christ possible, God willed his Church.* Indeed, the Church 'wishes to serve this single end: that each person may be able to find Christ, in order that Christ may walk with each person the path of life."[11] St. Paul VI was equally emphatic, teaching that "evangelizing all people constitutes the essential mission of the Church," and further that "evangelizing is in fact the grace and vocation proper to the Church, her deepest identity. She exists in order to evangelize."[12]

---

Landscape Study by Michael Lipka, "A closer look at America's rapidly growing religious 'nones'," Pew Research Center, May 13, 2015, http://www.pewresearch.org/fact-tank/2015/05/13/a-closer-look-at-americas-rapidly-growing-religious-nones/.

10 *Deus Caritas Est*, no 1.

11 *Veritatis Splendor*, no. 7 (emphasis in original).

12 *Evangelii Nuntiandi*, no. 14.

The new evangelization is "new" for a number of reasons. First, in the developed Western world, we are called to find new ways to engage and evangelize a post-Christian culture. Second, apostles and monks and nuns will not be the only ones spearheading this effort. This time, lay Christians and families are called to be at the forefront of this great endeavor, alongside the Church's religious and clergy.

### Families and "the Benedict Option"?

The recent book by Rod Dreher *The Benedict Option* has sparked much conversation in Catholic, Orthodox, and Protestant Christian circles.[13] Dreher confronts the post-Christian character of our culture head-on and parallels present day Western culture with the decay and decline of Rome. He advocates a "strategic retreat" from the increasingly secular culture around us and the cultivation of small Christian communities among families. For these communities, he draws principles and practices from the Rule of Saint Benedict, highlighting things like order, prayer, work, asceticism, stability, hospitality, and balance. The idea is to focus on cultivating and passing on the Christian faith to future generations in the midst of the new dark ages that have befallen us, just as the monastic communities founded by St. Benedict of Nursia did in his day.

Many of the ideas put forward in Dreher's book cohere with those in this book. We need to make our families a sanctuary or refuge from destructive influences in contemporary

---

13 *The Benedict Option: A Strategy for Christians in a Post-Christian Nation* (New York: Sentinel, 2017).

life. At the same time, we have to be intentional in developing practices that encourage the formation of children in the faith—things like order, prayer, shared work, certain forms of asceticism, and hospitality are as at home in family life as they are in monastic life and have been discussed in the preceding chapters. And families need the support of other families and the wider Christian community to flourish as cells within the body of Christ.

But there is one important qualifier regarding this "Benedict option." The "retreat" from the culture must be a "retreat in order to engage." As we have seen, families are called to be fully engaged in this effort. Indeed, the invocation of early medieval Europe, which was the context for Saint Benedict and his Rule, reinforces the point. These medieval monasteries were not isolated communities closed in on themselves, perfecting the practice of the virtues—they were centers of evangelization and education for the peoples around them. Like those communities, our families are called to give witness to those around us.

### Witness in Deeds

A famous saying often attributed to Saint Francis of Assisi states, "Preach the gospel always; use words when necessary." While we do not know that he said it, it captures an important truth: the way Christians live—their practices, behavior, and attitudes—make up a significant part of our witness to Christ. They give a baseline of credibility to our spoken witness. This is true in our families, as well. Families exercise the lead role in the Church's ministry to families "above all through their joy-filled witness as domestic churches." How do families do this?

Many decisions that we make regarding marriage and family life have become countercultural and therefore serve as acts of Christian witness. This begins with the decision to marry and the particulars of the wedding celebration. In a culture where the majority of people cohabit before marriage and fewer people marry, the decision to marry is a powerful affirmation of the goodness and value of marriage. The decision to marry in the Church and to prioritize sacramental marriage—as opposed, for example, to a destination wedding in some picturesque spot before a justice of the peace—heightens this witness. And the effort to push back against the growing commercialization and expense of weddings by striving to keep the celebration simple and prayerful reinforces the power of this witness.[14]

These decisions that start with the wedding should carry into the witness of the family. The homes of families who prioritize time for prayer and set boundaries on the noise of the media and technology feel different than those of their neighbors who may be more connected technologically but whose members are often less connected to one another. Families who make decisions to prioritize time together over money and material things and who choose to live more

14 In 2016, the popular wedding planning site *The Knot* estimated that the cost of weddings in the US had risen to over $35,000—significantly higher in urban areas. See Maggie Seaver, "The National Average Cost of a Wedding Hits $35,329," *The Knot*, accessed March 18, 2017, https://www.theknot.com/content/average-wedding-cost-2016.

simply, to practice hospitality, and to serve the disadvantaged stand out in their neighborhoods and communities.

This witness then creates the opportunity for sharing the faith with others. Those who encounter such families are often moved to ask, "Why do you that?" or "Why do you live this way?" This gives an opportunity for family members to "be ready to give an explanation to anyone who asks . . . a reason for . . . [their] hope" (cf. 1 Pt 3:15).

In an interview given at the beginning of his papacy, Pope Francis described the Church as a field hospital where those suffering from the wounds of sin (i.e., all of us) can encounter Christ and the healing he offers:

> The thing the church needs most today is the ability to heal wounds and to warm the hearts of the faithful; it needs nearness, proximity. I see the church as a field hospital after battle. It is useless to ask a seriously injured person if he has high cholesterol and about the level of his blood sugars! You have to heal his wounds. Then we can talk about everything else. Heal the wounds, heal the wounds. . . . And you have to start from the ground up.[15]

The Christian family too, as a domestic church, is a field hospital in which Christ is present in his ministry of healing. As its members encounter Christ and the healing power of grace in the sacraments and in their daily prayer and service, they become capable of inviting others in their communities

15 Pope Francis, from the Interview "A Big Heart Open to God," *America Magazine*, September 19, 2013. Cf. *Amoris Laetitia*, no. 291.

to this same healing encounter. They become orderlies of the Great Physician, assisting the wounded from the battlefield into the field hospital of the Church.

## Accompaniment and Family Witness

But how should this invitation to encounter Christ and his healing be made—especially by lay people and their families? After all, it is one thing for vowed religious or members of the clergy to do this. It is expected of them by virtue of their state in life. One might say that it's in their job description. But lay people with families are called to a different kind of life and witness.

There is no one answer to this question. Some families might feel called to devote themselves to missionary work in their own country or abroad. Others might devote themselves to a particular apostolate. Others might simply engage in a variety of ministries in their parish or elsewhere as a form of outreach. But how do families do this in the midst of their daily lives?

One way families can think about living out their call to missionary discipleship is through what Pope Francis calls "accompaniment." In *Evangelii Gaudium,* he describes the practice this way:

> Today more than ever we need men and women who, on the basis of their experience of accompanying others, are familiar with processes which call for prudence, understanding, patience and docility to the Spirit, so that they can protect the sheep from wolves who would scatter the flock. We need to practice the art of

> listening, which is more than simply hearing. Listening, in communication, is an openness of heart which makes possible that closeness without which genuine spiritual encounter cannot occur. Listening helps us to find the right gesture and word which shows that we are more than simply bystanders.
>
> Only through such respectful and compassionate listening can we enter on the paths of true growth and awaken a yearning for the Christian ideal: the desire to respond fully to God's love and to bring to fruition what he has sown in our lives.[16]

What Pope Francis provides here is a description of Christian friendship—people who walk with others, listen to them, share their lives. Such a friendship could be the basis of fellowship between two believers; it could take place within the context of spiritual direction, or it could be the basis of evangelization. If Christ is at the center of a person's life, then part of the sharing in this friendship will necessarily involve sharing about one's faith in him.

The idea of "accompaniment" was much discussed during the 2015 Synod on the Family at which John served. Many of the bishops and others attending the synod characterized accompaniment by referring to the biblical story of the disciples on the road to Emmaus (Lk 24:13–35). Jesus walked with these disciples and listened to their fears and frustrations. However, he did not simply leave them in their confusion. He challenged their lack of faith, broadened their

---

16 *Evangelii Gaudium*, no. 171.

understanding of Scripture, and ultimately revealed himself to them in the "breaking of the bread" which is the Eucharist.

How do we practice such accompaniment in the context of our family life? We do so by cultivating friendships with others—both individuals and families. This means sharing our lives with them, listening to them, and sharing our faith with them as we have the opportunity. It also means allowing others to share their faith and knowledge of God with us, and learning from them. For Christians, the goal of accompaniment is to invite those with whom we walk to deeper faith. Such deeper faith is always the work of the Holy Spirit in and among us. As Pope Paul VI noted, "It must be said that the Holy Spirit is the principal agent of evangelization: it is He who impels each individual to proclaim the Gospel, and it is He who in the depths of consciences causes the word of salvation to be accepted and understood."[17]

## Witnessing as a Family

Unlike some families we know and admire, we have never devoted ourselves to full-time missionary work or engaged in an apostolate as a family. Our witness as a family took other forms, most of them interwoven with our daily life and family practices.

As described in previous chapters, we did make certain decisions to prioritize family prayer, time together, and limiting the encroachments of the media and the consumer culture in our home. When guests visited our home for a meal or to stay for some period of time, they experienced

[17] *Evangelii Nuntiandi*, no. 75.

the way we lived and interacted. Some found it rather odd, and some found it inviting. When an adult friend of one of our children spent Christmas with us a few years ago, we included him in our family prayer, Christmas Mass, and the rest of our celebration of the Lord's nativity. Though he would describe himself as a "none" in his religious affiliation, he sent us a warm note of thanks after his visit, saying, "Thank you for sharing your family and your faith with me."

Of course, we've had our share of failures and struggles as a family which have challenged the coherence of our actions with our professed beliefs as Christians. One particular area of difficulty for us has been our finances. In spite of God's provision for us over the years—often miraculously—we often found ourselves struggling with worries about not being able to pay our bills. Jesus's exhortation in the Gospel not to worry about clothing, money, or possessions and to entrust ourselves to his Father's providence (see Mt 6:24–34) often seemed beyond the reach of our circumstances. As parents, we worried about the negative witness of this anxiety on our children (but worrying about worry did not resolve the issue!). We alternated being responsible for keeping track of our finances over the years, but that didn't fix the problem. Every month, we strained to pay our bills and to make ends meet, and we felt like the amount we were able to give to the Church and to charity was inadequate.

About eight years ago, we took a course on finances at our parish. It was based on the ministry of a well-known Evangelical Christian financial advisor and talk show host that many Catholic parishes have found helpful.[18] Two of our children took the course with us. We learned about doing a monthly budget together, prioritizing sacrificial giving, paying off debt, and saving. It made a significant difference in our life as a couple and a family. We no longer feel like our money simply happens to us; we are now able to be more intentional and consistent in charitable giving and saving. We were able to get rid of debt, except for our mortgage. We have an emergency fund to cover unexpected things like our furnace dying just before Christmas. When we had to replace a car, we were able to pay cash for it. This has not removed all of our financial anxieties, but it has certainly helped us and our children overcome some of the stress that money had generated in us. We are therefore better able to respond to Jesus's challenge to practice poverty of heart (Mt 5:3) and to resist having "two masters"—God and mammon (cf. Mt 6:24).

When it comes to giving witness through words, we are in a somewhat unique position because of John's occupation as a theologian. Talking about God is what he does for a living, so it was a natural and constant topic in our family. It has also spilled over into our shared ministries as a couple. Because of our love for marriage, we have prepared couples for marriage for about twenty-five years. Most of this ministry has been done in couple-to-couple formats in which we

18 The course we took was Dave Ramsey's Financial Peace University. Information about his books and courses can be found at Ramsey Solutions at www.daveramsey.com. Other churches have used programs developed by Larry Burkett. See Crown Financial Ministries, http://www.crown.org/.

have had couples come to our home in the months prior to their weddings. We have given talks together at parishes and conferences. And, as we have mentioned, for the last nine years, we have helped to run a post-Cana marriage ministry in our parish. All of this helped our children, as they were growing up, to see that sharing their faith is a normal part of Christian life. Though we never pushed or demanded it of them, our children, too, in their own ways and according to their own temperaments and gifts, looked for opportunities to do the same—serving as catechists, peer ministers, confirmation sponsors, and informal apologists among their peers.

The experience of one of our children provides an example of the practice of accompaniment outlined by Pope Francis. After a number of years of being homeschooled, our daughter returned to public school. There she became friends with a girl whose father is a pastor of a non-denominational Protestant church. The two friends supported one another in apologetic defenses of the faith in classes where skeptical students or teachers raised objections to Christian belief. At the same time, they had extensive conversations about differences in their own Christian belief and practice—as one might expect in the case where one child has a theologian for a parent and the other a pastor! The friendship continued through their high school and college years and beyond into graduate study in theology for our daughter's friend. Our daughter was present when her dear friend was received into the Catholic Church and subsequently served as the maid of honor at her wedding. These two friends gave and received over the years of their friendship and the result was a deeper embrace of their shared faith in Christ.

Claire and John have had a similar experience over the years in preparing couples for marriage. At times, we have had couples offer to pay us for our time. We explain to them that accompanying another couple as they prepare for the sacrament of marriage builds up our own marriage and deepens our faith. That is all the payment we need. Faith is not a zero-sum game. It actually increases the more we share it with others.

**Key Points**

- Like the Church, Christian families are called to evangelize.
- In our day, the Church and all of her members are called to be active participants in the New Evangelization.
- Christians are called to give witness in deeds as well as through words.
- Families can engage in this Christian witness through the practice of accompaniment.

11

# Letting Go: Surrendering Our Children to God

As parents of four college graduates and a current college student, we have become aware, over the years, of the term "helicopter parents." College administrators and staff use this term to describe parents who bring their children to campus at the beginning of their freshman year and then have a difficult time leaving. They might decide to stay nearby beyond orientation and even into the first week of classes just in case their child might need something from them. When they reluctantly—and perhaps tearfully—head home, they are already making plans for their next visit, usually long before parents weekend. They struggle to adjust to having their child away from home and feel certain that he or she cannot flourish without their presence and caretaking activity.

In some families, this phenomenon persists beyond the college years. Parents can have a difficult time accepting the fact that their children have become adults and adjusting their relationships accordingly. Such behavior can foster a lack of responsibility or immaturity in adult children. Of course, adult children might need additional support from their parents for legitimate reasons such as illness, job loss, or help with college debt. And certainly, sometimes the resistance to assuming adult responsibilities can come from the children themselves with no unhealthy enabling on the part of their parents. But clearly, the norm is that the relationship between parents and children changes as young men and women transition from adolescence to adulthood, and this is a good thing.

Our task as parents is to do our best to form our children into men and women who are capable of discerning God's call to them and responding to it generously. As children enter into adulthood, however, they assume responsibility for their own growth and ongoing formation as Christians. They are also responsible for discerning God's call to them, including his call to particular states of life—marriage, religious life, or priesthood.

We began the book by reflecting on the biblical invitation to see our children as gifts from God and to realize that they are more his children than ours. As they move into adulthood, therefore, we are called to entrust them to God and allow them to pursue his will and plan for their lives. We surrender them; however, we don't abandon them. That is, although we surrender the control of their lives and the responsibility for their decisions to them, we are careful never to turn our backs on them. Accompaniment in love, prayer, mutual support, and friendship ought to continue in these reconfigured family relationships. Even if a child rejects his or her faith or family, Christian parents are called (like the father in the parable of the Prodigal Son—cf. Lk 15:11–32) to keep the doors of the relationship open in the hope of a future reconciliation. Knowing the great mercy God has shown to us enables us to extend mercy toward others (cf. Col 3:12–13), even in the face of family estrangement.

## Parental Surrender in the Scriptures

Scripture provides us with many examples of parents who prioritized responding to God's call over seeking their own happiness in and through their children. We have already spoken of Hannah who prayed desperately for a child and then, on having her prayer answered, dedicated her child to God after he was weaned by leaving him to be raised by the priests of Israel's temple (1 Sm 1, see esp. v. 28). But Abraham and Mary, two great biblical models of faith, provide the preeminent examples of parental relinquishment.

Jews, Christians, and Muslims see Abraham as a model of faith. St. Paul tells the Christians of Galatia that if they belong to Christ through Baptism, then they have Abraham as their father (cf. Gal 3:29). For Christians of Gentile origin, this was not because of physical descent from Abraham (cf. Rom 4:1, 12). Rather, he is a model for us precisely in his faith and the fact that this faith—and not circumcision or following the law—put him in right relationship with God (i.e., caused him to be justified; cf. Rom 4:2–3, 9–14). Like Abraham, we are called to believe, and this assent to God's gift of faith in Christ is what puts us in right relationship with him (cf. Rom 4:22–25).

But the circumstances of Abraham's belief are worth pondering further. St. Paul writes, "He did not weaken in faith when he considered his own body as [already] dead (for he was almost a hundred years old) and the dead womb of Sarah" (Rom 4:19). According to Genesis (17:1, 17), Abraham was ninety-nine years old and Sarah was ninety when God promised them a son who would be the heir of God's covenant promise and the father of a great nation. In spite of some initial incredulity,[1] Abraham and Sarah believed God and did conceive Isaac in their old age as the Lord had promised them (Gn 21:1–5). It is in this context of the realization of God's improbable covenant promise that Abraham's faith is subjected to a further test.

In Genesis 22, Abraham is told to take Isaac—his only son by Sarah and the one he was told would be the heir of all of God's promises—and offer him in sacrifice on a mountain in the distant land of Moriah (vv. 1–2). Later biblical tradition would identify this height with the mount on which the Jerusalem temple would be built (cf. 2 Chr 3:1). Abraham dutifully set out to obey this wrenching directive from the Lord, but an angel stopped him in the very act of carrying it out (see Gn 22:11–12). Some of the peoples of the ancient Near East practiced child sacrifice, so as shocking as God's command might sound to our ears, it would not have seemed so improbable to Abraham.

Some biblical scholars read this text as a breakthrough moment in which ancient Israel came to understand that

---

1 Both Abraham and Sarah's initial reactions were laughter in the face of this seemingly impossible promise (see Gn 17:17; 18:12). We might also note their effort to engineer the realization of this promise through their own efforts in bringing about the birth of Ishmael in Genesis 16.

Yahweh was not a God who desired human sacrifice.[2] Yet even in later biblical thought, there was an understanding that firstborn sons belong to God and had to be redeemed by other means (cf. Ex 13:11–16; 34:19–20). For Jewish and Christian readers of Scripture, the story of "the binding of Isaac" (cf. Gn 22:9) is a uniquely powerful testament to Abraham's faith resting in God rather than in what seemed to be the tangible realization of God's promise to himself and his family. He was literally willing to surrender his son and all of his hopes for him to God. For Christians, this foreshadows God's gift of his firstborn Son on our behalf in the establishment of the New Covenant out of love for fallen humanity (cf. Rom 8:32).

In the pages of the New Testament, we meet a still more powerful model of faith on the part of a parent who plays a pivotal role in salvation history—the mother of Jesus. Even more than Abraham and Sarah, Mary's conception of a child is the result of God's gracious intervention and her own ready assent of faith (cf. Lk 1:35, 38). Though the angel's words trouble her (Lk 1:29), she does not laugh as Abraham and Sarah did, nor doubt as did John the Baptist's father, Zechariah (cf. Lk 1:20). Instead, Mary accepts the Lord's word to her, rejoices in God's mighty deeds, and "ponders" the events of her Son's life "in her heart" (cf. Lk 2:19, 51). She is present at the wedding feast of Cana where her Son performs his first "sign" in response to her intercession on behalf of the unfortunate family who had run out of wine (cf. Jn 2:1–11).

---

2 See Miller, "A Biblical Charter of Children's Rights: Genesis 22," *Biblical Faith and Fathering*, pp. 137–41.

Yet, though she, like the disciples, beheld Jesus's glory in this and other signs, Mary's faith grew over time as she came to understand her Son and his mission more fully.[3]

Like Abraham, Mary's faith was subjected to a still more painful and difficult test. Unlike Abraham, who did not have to sacrifice his son, Mary, at the cross, beholds her Son's public rejection and execution by his own people and the governing Roman authorities. Mary's faith is put to the greatest test—it seems that everything she had hoped and believed about her Son was being taken from her. Simeon's prophecy that a "sword would pierce" Mary's heart (cf. Lk 2:35) finds its bitter fulfillment in the passion of the Lord. Yet even in this dark hour, she is given a further mission by her Son, being assigned as "mother" to the Beloved Disciple (a model for all Christians in the fourth Gospel; cf. Jn 19:26). Mary, too, beholds the glory of her Son's resurrection and is present with the apostles in the Upper Room, praying for the coming of the Holy Spirit at Pentecost.

The surrender faced by most Christian parents may not be as painful and certainly will not be as pivotal in salvation history as those which Abraham and Mary were called to undertake, yet it is a real part of our vocation as parents. As our children progress through infancy to childhood to adolescence to adulthood, we slowly give them more autonomy, recognizing their need to make their own decisions and then holding them accountable for them and their consequences. In so doing, we hope and pray that the formation which we

---

3 For a beautiful, biblical meditation on Mary's growth in faith as a disciple, see St. John Paul II's 1987 encyclical *Redmptoris Mater*.

have helped provide enables them to continue to make good choices, to pursue virtuous friendships with others, and to prioritize knowing God and his plan for their lives.

But we do not control these choices and their outcomes. Instead, we entrust our children to God and his great love and mercy and—bit by bit—we learn to let go. Sometimes this surrender takes a painful and unexpected turn when our children make bad decisions about the direction of their lives or reject their family or even their faith. Some parents face the agony of losing a child to death. But even without the dark night of such painful events, we are called to place our children in the hands of the God who created them. Having helped to form our children as best we can, we allow them to follow the Lord and their conscience.

### Forming Consciences

As we have seen, our families are places of formation. Husbands and wives form one another, parents form their children, especially in their younger years, and children also form their parents, especially as they mature in their faith as Christians. By teaching our children to love, to forgive, to serve, and to pray, we are really helping to form their conscience so that they can hear and respond to God's call to them.

Many people do not realize that there is more to conscience formation than religious education or catechesis. It is certainly important that our children learn the truths of their faith from us, as their parents, and from others—priests, catechists, teachers. It is important that they learn to read Scripture, study the Catechism, and, as they mature, learn where to go for resources to guide their own further study and formation. But all of this yields only what St. John Paul II calls "objective moral knowledge."[4] This is what we might call "head knowledge." It is information that we have learned and committed to memory. It has not yet been appropriated on a deeper level.

Real moral knowledge that genuinely informs our conscience is knowledge that we have personally appropriated through prayer, through suffering, through action, and through love (i.e., through the experience of Christian living). Such information is more "caught" than "taught." It impacts our imaginations and engages our hearts—not simply our memory or intellect. This is information that has become part of our character. In other words, it is habituated knowledge or virtue.[5] This is where conscience is genuinely formed. The practices that we undertake as Christian families—in how we pray, how we communicate, how we eat, how we serve, how we reconcile, how we recreate—are among the most formative influences in our children's lives and consciences.

When we are confronted with an important decision, we draw on the deep capacity we have to hear and respond to God, the moral knowledge we have acquired and made our own, and we make a decision: "I should do x" or "God wants me to do x." Such a particular judgment of conscience is morally binding—but only on the person who makes

---

4 See John Paul II, encyclical *Veritatis Splendor*, no. 63.

5 See Ibid., no. 64.

it. It is not transferable to others—even those in identical circumstances. St. John Paul II calls a particular judgment of conscience a "proximate norm."[6] We cannot impose our judgment of what God's will is for us on other people. This is what Pope Francis means when he says, "We have been called to form consciences, not to replace them."[7]

Parents make basic decisions for very young children to teach them what is good and bad, but as children mature, we give them more freedom and allow them to make more decisions for themselves. A toddler might be taught to always hold an adult's hand while crossing a street or while in a parking lot. A grade school child might be frequently exhorted to look both ways when crossing the street. A teenager with a driver's license might be given a curfew and guidance about where and with whom he or she might go. We still hold older children accountable when they make bad decisions, but their autonomy in making their own decisions expands over time. A similar progression takes place in the moral sphere with issues like telling the truth, respect for other people, relating to others chastely, the practice of justice, and care for the environment.

## Hearing the Call

When it comes to our children's discernment of things like a state in life, the choice of a spouse, or the selection of a profession, we respect our children's ability to hear and respond to God's call to them. We might have ideas and opinions in

---

6 See Ibid., no. 60.

7 *Amoris Laetitia*, no. 37.

such matters, and typically have some opportunity to share them in appropriate ways. However, we cannot hear God on behalf of our adult children. We cannot substitute our judgment for theirs.

When our children have done their best to seek God's will for their lives, our role is to support and encourage them in responding to what they believe is God's will. If we thought a child might have a religious vocation but instead decides to marry, we should encourage him or her to prepare accordingly. Conversely, we might think one of our children would make a wonderful spouse and parent and be surprised by his or her decision to enter religious life. The lives of the saints are filled with examples of children who entered religious life over the objections of their parents. If a child marries someone who, in our opinion, is not the best match, our role is to do whatever we can to help that marriage flourish. Parental insight cannot trump God's call.[8] Our children need the freedom to respond to God.

There are cases where we might feel called to warn or challenge our children when we see them making what we believe to be a mistake. When they are in love with someone and considering marriage but everyone around them sees red flags, we might feel, in conscience, compelled to honestly and charitably express our reservations. Pope Francis says that one successful outcome of good marriage preparation is to help couples who should not be getting married

---

8 Even in cultures where parents or families play a role in arranging a marriage, the Church insists on the free consent of the couple for the validity of the sacrament.

to arrive at that discernment and decision together.[9] Such warnings are sometimes better received from people outside of the family than within it (priests or mentor couples), but in some cases, parents are in a position to appropriately register their concerns. It is better to risk hurt feelings in the honest expression of concern than to endure the heartbreak and trauma of divorce later.

Sometimes parents know that adult children are making choices that are not God's will for them. For example, when a young adult couple opt for cohabitation. In this case, the parents' task is to "speak the truth in love" (cf. Eph 4:15) and to state their objections.

But does this violate what was said above about not trying to replace the consciences of our adult children? No, because in this case we have an example of young adults who are either not following their consciences or acting on consciences which have been formed badly. God never directs people to do what is objectively wrong. Scripture and the Church's tradition bear consistent witness to the moral evil of sex outside of the covenant of marriage. This perennial wisdom is confirmed by social scientific research that has found that cohabitation prior to marriage is a major predictor of later marital failure. Sexual cohabitation sabotages the success of that future marriage and undermines the happiness which the couple seeks for their relationship.[10] Warning

---

9 See *Amoris Laetitia*, no. 209.

10 On the reasons why cohabitation sabotages later marital success, see the USCCB statement "Marriage Preparation and Cohabiting Couples" (1999), http://www.usccb.org/issues-and-action/marriage-and-family/marriage/marriage-preparation/cohabiting.cfm.

or correcting another person when he or she makes bad moral choices is part of our responsibility and stems from sharing in the prophetic office (cf. Ez 33:1–20) and from being members of the body of Christ (cf. Mt 18:15–17).

Of course, responding to God's call by choosing marriage or religious life is different from choosing something that is objectively evil. In the former, a person is choosing a path in order to realize a good: "How does God want me to grow in holiness?" or "How am I called to love my neighbor?" These are positive—not negative—directives given to all of us as members of the Church. Only the individual Christian in the depths of his or her own heart can discern God's call to live out their baptismal vocation in a specific state in life. Having done our best to lead our children to encounter the Lord and learn to follow him, our job is to echo to them the words of the Blessed Mother to the servants at the Wedding Feast of Cana: "Do whatever he tells you" (Jn 2:5).

### Key Points

- As our children move into adulthood, we are called to surrender them to God but not abandon them.
- Abraham and Mary are models of what parental surrender to God looks like.
- As parents, we are called to help form our children's conscience both by handing on the faith to them and helping them to internalize it through practices.

---

See also the excellent essay by Cassandra Hough, "The Fullness of Sexuality: Church Teaching on Premarital Sex," in *Women, Sex, and the Church: A Case for Catholic Teaching*, Erika Bachiochi, ed. (Boston: Pauline, 2012), 57–78.

- Ultimately, our children have to hear and respond to God's call to them to a particular state of life; our role as parents is to support and encourage them.

12

# Conclusion: Formation Beyond the Vows

In Scripture, weddings are often used to symbolize fulfillment or completion. In the Gospels, Jesus is described as the bridegroom who brings God's kingdom (see Mk 2:19; Mt 9:15; Lk 5:34; Jn 3:29). In such teaching, he re-expresses the covenant symbolism used to describe the relationship between God and the people of Israel in the Old Testament (cf. Hos 2:16–22; Is 54:5–6; 62:5; Ez 16:6–14). Jesus's parables challenge us to be prepared for his coming through using the image of a wedding (cf. Mt 22:1–14; Lk 14:15–24; Mt 25:1–13). Heaven is described in the New Testament as "the wedding feast of the Lamb" (cf. Rv 19:6–9) which completes the union of Jesus the bridegroom with his bride, the Church (cf. Eph 5:22–27).

This image is apt and draws on the natural symbolism of a wedding as the fulfillment of human hopes. After all, men and women may search for years to find the right person to whom they can commit themselves for life. The joy of the couple is usually shared by family and friends who desire their happiness and gather to celebrate this culmination of their hopes and dreams. This joy is shared in a particular way by parents who hope, pray, and work for the happiness of their children.

Having recently celebrated the wedding of our son, we are also cognizant of the fact that a wedding represents the culmination of a long process of planning—actually a number of processes. There is the preparation of the couple, the planning of the liturgy, the composition of the guest list, and the planning of the reception with its myriad of details. Even couples and families who strive for simplicity in the wedding celebration, as Pope Francis recommends, can find themselves exhausted at its culmination.

Yet, rightly understood, weddings mark a beginning much more than they do an end. The call to holiness received in Baptism is now re-specified by the entrance into this new state in life and the need to learn what it means to lay down one's life in love for one's spouse and, later, one's children. The newly married person is both expected and capacitated by the sacrament to love, serve, and witness in new ways. More than a finish line, weddings represent a starting line for the next leg of the race which is the Christian life (cf. 1 Cor 9:24; 2 Tm 4:7).

This fact is important in a culture such as ours. In the past, couples entering marriage could count on the support of the extended family and the parish community to support and sustain them, and the wider culture to backstop them in providing basic moral formation for their children. As we have seen, these supports can no longer be presumed. In many ways, the Church was slow to recognize these cultural changes and the new pressures on Christian families. This meant, in some sense, that couples were "turned loose" after their wedding. It was almost as if the newly married were given the message: "Have a nice life! Don't forget to bring your kids back to have them baptized!" Cast adrift in an increasingly secularized culture, many younger families simply stopped practicing their faith.

It is clear from the Church's recent teaching that her pastors recognize that this approach no longer works. As we saw in chapter 6, the Church has begun to emphasize the need for ongoing formation and accompaniment of couples after the celebration of their wedding.[1] This is uncharted territory for those who do marriage and family ministry, but it is vital for families if they are to be able to fulfill their vocations and mission in our present culture. As noted previously, this kind of post-Cana formation is not the focus of this book, but it is crucial to understand that it is necessary.

As parents, our role in our children's lives does not end with their wedding any more than it ends at the door of the convent or seminary in the case of a child with a religious or priestly vocation. It does change, however. The newly married couple now constitute a family themselves—as man and wife, they are "one flesh," in the words of the author of Genesis 2:24. We must recognize and support them as such.

But just because adult children leave our homes, that does not mean that they leave our hearts or lives. As we saw in the last chapter, surrendering our children to God does not mean abandoning them. We continue to accompany them with our prayers, love, encouragement, and example. We

---

1 This was mentioned by Pope John Paul II in *Familiaris Consortio*, no. 69. It is treated extensively by Pope Francis in *Amoris Laetitia*, nos. 217–30.

offer our own experience when asked or when the opportunity presents itself. We hope that they will continue to learn from us and we will continue to learn from them. When we continue to share our lives in the midst of these changed roles and relationships, we discover that family is a much richer and wider reality than simply the nuclear family of parents and children. As Pope Francis says, "The nuclear family needs to interact with the wider family made up of parents, aunts and uncles, cousins and even neighbors. This greater family may have members who require assistance, or at least companionship and affection, or consolation amid suffering. The individualism so prevalent today can lead to creating small nests of security, where others are perceived as bothersome or a threat. Such isolation, however, cannot offer greater peace or happiness; rather, it straitens the heart of a family and makes its life all the more narrow."[2]

In addition to this ongoing accompaniment and support, parents can encourage their married children to seek further formation. In some cases, parents may be able to supply some of this formation. In other cases, they may not. However, they can certainly supply their own example in looking for such formation themselves. In our post-Cana marriage ministry, we have been edified by the example of couples married nearly twice as long as ourselves who have taken our formation classes and shared some of their own wisdom with younger couples in the group. Such couples demonstrate to us that one is never too old to learn or to teach others what it means to respond more fully to God's call.

---

2 *Amoris Laetitia*, no. 187.

Whether they are adults or newborns, our children are in truth God's children. God knows and has a plan for each one before his or her birth (cf. Jer 1:5). Each person is utterly unique and is called by God in a personal and distinct manner. The most important thing we can do as parents is to form our children as best we can to be capable of hearing and responding to his call. None of us does this perfectly. But the grace of God can overcome and even work through our weaknesses and failures. The key is to order the daily life and practices of our homes and families so as to be receptive to that grace and to encounter the One who is its source.

God's call to us is not only profoundly personal; it is also intrinsically social. God calls us in families and God calls us as families. As the Body of Christ, united by Baptism, the Church is also herself the family of God. As God's family, we listen for his voice as he says to us each and to us all: "Do not fear, for I have redeemed you; I have called you by name: you are mine" (Is 43:1).

### Key Points

- A wedding is a time of fulfillment of many hopes and dreams, but it is also a beginning.
- Couples need ongoing support, formation, and accompaniment beyond their wedding.
- Parents and adult children can continue to form one another even after children marry or enter religious life.